JUSTICE IN THE BALANCE
Recommendations for an Independent and Effective International Criminal Court

Human Rights Watch
New York · Washington · London · Brussels

ISBN:1-56432-184-3
Library of Congress Catalog Card Number: 98-86246

Addresses for Human Rights Watch
350 Fifth Avenue, 34th Floor, New York, NY 10118-3299
Tel: (212) 290-4700, Fax: (212) 736-1300, E-mail: hrwnyc@hrw.org

1522 K Street, N.W., #910, Washington, DC 20005-1202
Tel: (202) 371-6592, Fax: (202) 371-0124, E-mail: hrwdc@hrw.org

33 Islington High Street, N1 9LH London, UK
Tel: (171) 713-1995, Fax: (171) 713-1800, E-mail: hrwatchuk@gn.apc.org

15 Rue Van Campenhout, 1000 Brussels, Belgium
Tel: (2) 732-2009, Fax: (2) 732-0471, E-mail: hrwatcheu@gn.apc.org

Web Site Address: http://www.hrw.org

Listserv address: To subscribe to the list, send an e-mail message to
majordomo@igc.apc.org with "subscribe hrw-news" in the body of the message
(leave the subject line blank).

Human Rights Watch is dedicated to
protecting the human rights of people around the world.

We stand with victims and activists to prevent
discrimination, to uphold political freedom, to protect people from
inhumane conduct in wartime, and to bring offenders to justice.

We investigate and expose
human rights violations and hold abusers accountable.

We challenge governments and those who hold power to end
abusive practices and respect international human rights law.

We enlist the public and the international
community to support the cause of human rights for all.

HUMAN RIGHTS WATCH

Human Rights Watch conducts regular, systematic investigations of human rights abuses in some seventy countries around the world. Our reputation for timely, reliable disclosures has made us an essential source of information for those concerned with human rights. We address the human rights practices of governments of all political stripes, of all geopolitical alignments, and of all ethnic and religious persuasions. Human Rights Watch defends freedom of thought and expression, due process and equal protection of the law, and a vigorous civil society; we document and denounce murders, disappearances, torture, arbitrary imprisonment, discrimination, and other abuses of internationally recognized human rights. Our goal is to hold governments accountable if they transgress the rights of their people.

Human Rights Watch began in 1978 with the founding of its Europe and Central Asia division (then known as Helsinki Watch). Today, it also includes divisions covering Africa, the Americas, Asia, and the Middle East. In addition, it includes three thematic divisions on arms, children's rights, and women's rights. It maintains offices in New York, Washington, Los Angeles, London, Brussels, Moscow, Dushanbe, Rio de Janeiro, and Hong Kong. Human Rights Watch is an independent, nongovernmental organization, supported by contributions from private individuals and foundations worldwide. It accepts no government funds, directly or indirectly.

The staff includes Kenneth Roth, executive director; Michele Alexander, development director; Reed Brody, advocacy director; Carroll Bogert, communications director; Cynthia Brown, program director; Barbara Guglielmo, finance and administration director; Jeri Laber special advisor; Lotte Leicht, Brussels office director; Patrick Minges, publications director; Susan Osnos, associate director; Jemera Rone, counsel; Wilder Tayler, general counsel; and Joanna Weschler, United Nations representative. Jonathan Fanton is the chair of the board. Robert L. Bernstein is the founding chair.

The regional directors of Human Rights Watch are Peter Takirambudde, Africa; José Miguel Vivanco, Americas; Sidney Jones, Asia; Holly Cartner, Europe and Central Asia; and Hanny Megally, Middle East and North Africa. The thematic division directors are Joost R. Hiltermann, arms; Lois Whitman, children's; and Dorothy Q. Thomas, women's.

The members of the board of directors are Jonathan Fanton, chair; Lisa Anderson, Robert L. Bernstein, William Carmichael, Dorothy Cullman, Gina Despres, Irene Diamond, Adrian W. DeWind, Fiona Druckenmiller, Edith Everett, James C. Goodale, Jack Greenberg, Vartan Gregorian, Alice H. Henkin, Stephen L. Kass, Marina Pinto Kaufman, Bruce Klatsky, Harold Hongju Koh, Alexander MacGregor, Josh Mailman, Samuel K. Murumba, Andrew Nathan, Jane Olson, Peter Osnos, Kathleen Peratis, Bruce Rabb, Sigrid Rausing, Anita Roddick, Orville Schell, Sid Sheinberg, Gary G. Sick, Malcolm Smith, Domna Stanton, Maureen White, and Maya Wiley. Robert L. Bernstein is the founding chair of Human Rights Watch.

CONTENTS

ACKNOWLEDGMENTS

This report was written by Helen Duffy, counsel with Human Rights Watch. Valuable contributions were made by Phyllis Hwang, advocate, Richard Dicker, associate counsel, Yodon Thondon and Vikram Parekh of the Children's Rights Division, of Human Rights Watch. It was edited by Wilder Tayler, general counsel, Dinah PoKempner, deputy general counsel and Michael McClintock, deputy programme director of Human Rights Watch. Matthew McGowan prepared the report for publication and Clare Mumford and Laura Brav provided production assistance.

The writer is grateful to the many students and academics who assisted in the research of this report, in particular Professor Gregory Fox, Rhodri Williams, Lisa Laplante, Benjamin Rader, Matthew Griffin, Wiebke Ruckert, Jeremy Sharpe, Munir Pujara, Vijaya Gadde, Nanina Takla, Paul Martin, Margaret deGuzman, Shena Majeed, Nirupa Narayan, Mayur Subbarao, Jeremy Telman, Reka Ludanyi, Claudine Meredith-Goujon, Julia Rogers, Anne Bodley and Sara Stapleton.

I. INTRODUCTION

The diplomatic conference to establish the International Criminal Court (ICC) is potentially the most significant treaty conference in decades. Almost fifty years after the International Law Commission first concluded that the establishment of an ICC was possible and desirable, delegations have the opportunity to take this crucial and urgently needed step in the enforcement of human rights and humanitarian law. The work of the conference will be assessed by scholars, diplomats, and the public at large well into the next century. Its success will be judged not by whether a treaty emerges from the conference, but whether the institution it creates has the qualities essential to the fulfilment of its critical mandate.

The potential impact of the ICC is enormous. By holding individuals personally accountable, the Court could be an extremely powerful deterrent to the commission of genocide, crimes against humanity and serious war crimes that have plagued humanity during the course of this century. Not only is the establishment of the Court an opportunity to provide critical redress to victims and survivors, but potentially to spare victims from the horrors of such atrocities in the future. If effective, the ICC will extend the rule of law internationally, impelling national systems to themselves investigate and prosecute the most heinous crimes-- thus strengthening those systems-- while guaranteeing that where they fail, the ICC can operate to ensure that justice prevails over impunity. Human Rights Watch urges delegates meeting in Rome not to forfeit this historic opportunity.

If the ICC is to realize this potential, it must, like any credible judicial institution, be independent, fair and effective. At the outset of the Diplomatic Conference, key questions remain in the balance. Will the Court be created with the independence critical to its judicial function; or will it be saddled with an inherent susceptibility to political manipulation by states or the Security Council? Will it be a universal court, with jurisdiction to prosecute egregious crimes wherever and by whomever committed; or will particular states be given the right to unilaterally prevent justice in particular cases? Will it have jurisdiction over a full range of serious crimes; or have a restrictive jurisdiction, excluded from the prosecution of the crimes of most relevance in the modern world? Will states be clearly obliged to comply with the Court's requests and give effect to its judgments, or be entitled to select when to do so and when not? Will the Court observe the highest standards of international justice for suspects and accused persons, and for victims and witnesses; or will it lack legitimacy as an institution charged with the enforcement of international law?

While there is a multitude of complex and overlapping issues involved in these negotiations, we believe that the following seven benchmarks must be met if the ICC is to be an independent, fair and effective judicial institution.

1)   The jurisdictional regime must exclude any requirement of state consent. The decision to eliminate the opt-in/opt-out acceptance of jurisdiction over particular crimes, and consent on a case-by-case basis, is the most fundamental choice the conference must make. Requiring state consent would paralyze the Court. It would seriously undermine its independence and credibility.

2)   The Court must be independent of the Security Council or any other political body. No court which is seen as an arm of the Security Council will enjoy the credibility it needs to operate effectively. While the Security Council has an important role in referring cases to the Court, it should not be given control of the Court's docket. Virtually every delegation, except four Permanent Members, see Security Council veto over the exercise of the Court's jurisdiction as unacceptable political interference in the exercise of a judicial function.

3)   The Court must have an independent prosecutor. He or she must be empowered to initiate investigations on his or her own, in the light of information from any reliable source. In the face of evidence from victims and witnesses, the prosecutor must not be precluded from pursuing an investigation because a state or the Security Council did not do so. If the ICC can only investigate in the light of state complaints or Security Council referrals, it will be dependent on the political motivation of states and the Security Council for the execution of its judicial mandate. Experience demonstrates the reluctance of states to use existing state complaint procedures in human rights mechanisms. Ex *officio* prosecutorial powers are indispensable to the Court's practical impact and to its independence and legitimacy.

4)   The complementarity principle should ensure that the Court will not operate as a supranational institution with the power to substitute itself for national legal systems, but that the ICC is able to investigate and prosecute when national systems fail to do so. The impetus for the establishment of the ICC is the failure of national systems to hold the perpetrators of genocide, crimes against humanity, and war crimes accountable. Unqualified deference to state claims of jurisdiction, without appropriate ICC review and the power to take necessary measures to preserve evidence, will jeopardize the prospect of justice.

5)   The ICC must be able to prosecute those responsible for serious war crimes, whether committed in international or internal armed conflicts. The Court's jurisdiction over serious war crimes, is critical to its impact and credibility. In particular, if the ICC is to be relevant and effective in the contemporary world, in which the vast majority of conflicts are non-international, it must have sufficiently broad jurisdiction over crimes committed in this context.

6)   The statute must clearly establish the obligation on state parties to comply with requests from the Court, and prohibit unilateral refusal to do so. As the ICC will be entirely reliant on states to carry out indispensable investigative and enforcement functions, cooperation from states and compliance with its requests is essential. While the statute should make provision for dealing with legitimate concerns, such as serious national security concerns, the Court must retain ultimate authority to determine whether an exception to the general rule should be made in any concrete case.

7)   The ICC must respect the rights of the suspects and accused persons enshrined in international human rights instruments, and take measures to protect witnesses that testify before the Court.

This commentary focuses on key issues to be resolved at the ICC Diplomatic Conference. It is not exhaustive, but deals with matters which remain particularly critical or contentious. The commentaries prepared by Human Rights Watch for the April 1997, December 1997 and March 1998 preparatory committee sessions address additional issues. Each section of this commentary begins with introductory remarks and offers specific recommendations for the relevant articles of the current draft statute for the International Criminal Court (ICC). The recommendations are followed by comments that explain our underlying reasoning.

This document should be read together with the articles of the current draft statute (UN Doc.A/CONF.183/2/Add.1) to which they relate. Due to the length of the draft statute and the number of options in certain parts of the text, it was not possible to reproduce the text in this document. Alongside the article numbers of the current consolidated text, we have included in brackets the reference to the article number in the earlier draft text (referred to as the "Zutphen" text).

Human Rights Watch looks forward to working with the delegations attending the Diplomatic Conference, and to assisting any delegation. We expect that the partnership that has evolved between nongovernmental organizations and government delegations during the preparatory phase will develop and consolidate during this final critical stage.

SECTION A: THE SUBJECT MATTER JURISDICTION OF THE COURT

Article 5

The International Criminal Court should have jurisdiction over the most serious crimes of concern to the international community. In this document we will focus on two critical aspects of the subject matter jurisdiction of the Court which have given rise to considerable controversy in the course of debate during the Preparatory Committee. These are firstly the scope of the Court's jurisdiction over war crimes, in particular those committed in the context of non-international armed conflicts, and secondly the definition of crimes against humanity.

Part 1: WAR CRIMES

Summary of Section A, Part 1.
The recommendations and comments in this section comprise four parts. In (a) we set out the principles which should frame the negotiations around the scope of the Court's jurisdiction over war crimes. Contained in (b) is the list of war crimes which should be included, at a minimum, within that jurisdiction, for both international and non-international conflicts. Comments on the importance of including these basic crimes, and on the current text of the statute before the Diplomatic Conference, follow the recommendations. In (c) we recommend that the Court should have jurisdiction over other crimes that may come to form part of customary international law in the future, and in (d) we make recommendations on the options relating to a possible threshold limiting the Court's jurisdiction to crimes committed pursuant to a plan or policy, or on a massive scale.

The Structure of the War Crimes section of the draft statute
The part of Article 5 of the current draft statute which deals with the definition of war crimes is divided into four sections: section A, grave breaches, section B, other war crimes committed in international conflict, section C, violations of Common Article 3 of the Geneva Conventions, and section D, other war crimes committed in non-international armed conflicts. The division of international and non-international conflicts mirrors the distinction enshrined in humanitarian treaty law. This distinction, which exists as a result of the historical context from which the

treaties emerged, is becoming increasingly blurred as humanitarian law develops.[1] The statute, in creating an institution for the future, should reflect this trend and establish the Court's jurisdiction over serious war crimes, in line with the list in Section A, Part 1 (b) of this document, whether committed in internal or international conflicts.

GUIDING PRINCIPLES

International and non-international distinction

The statute should ensure that the Court has jurisdiction over serious war crimes, irrespective of whether they were committed in internal or international conflicts. Since the end of the Second World War, the vast majority of armed conflicts have been non-international.[2] It is in the course of such conflicts that some of the gravest violations of human rights and humanitarian law have occurred. The Court's very relevance in the contemporary world will hinge in large part on its ability to reflect this reality. The scope of the Court's jurisdiction over war crimes, and in particular its ability to prosecute those responsible for serious crimes in internal armed conflicts, is therefore critical to its impact and credibility.[3]

There should not be differential standards of criminal responsibility, and corresponding differential protection of victims, for the same conduct on the basis of the nature of the armed conflicts in which it was carried out.[4] This principle is

---

[1] See the United Nations "Minimum Humanitarian Standards: analytical report of the Secretary-General submitted pursuant to Commission on Human Rights resolution 1997/21," E/CN.4/1998/87, adopted by the United Nations Commission on Human Rights (Resolution 1998/29).

[2] Para.18 of U.N. "Minimum humanitarian standards."

[3] In 1995, according to the Stockholm Institute for Peace Research (SIPRI), *all* of the major armed conflicts around the world were internal. This fact remained unchanged from 1994. *SIPRI Yearbook*, (1996), p.15.

[4] Human Rights Watch in principle would support the creation of one list of crimes, without distinction as to the nature of the conflict within which the crimes are committed. What is essential, however, is that the crimes contained in Section A, Part 1 (b) of this document are included as a minimum, with respect to internal as well as international conflicts, for the reasons explained below.

reinforced by the factual difficulty that often arises in determining whether a conflict is international or non-international for the purposes of making such a legal distinction.[5]

Although the express duty to prosecute under the Geneva Conventions arises only with respect to grave breaches in international conflicts,[6] international law has developed to the point where it is now established that individuals are criminally responsible for serious violations of humanitarian law committed in internal conflicts.[7] This is clearly set out in the decision of the International Criminal Tribunal for the Former Yugoslavia (ICTY) in the case of *Prosecutor v. Tadic*.[8] The approach of the tribunal is also reflected in United Nations Security Council resolutions in recent years which, in addition to categorizing civil wars as matters

---

[5] One example was the conflict in Vietnam, which had some of the characteristics of international armed conflict and some of civil war. See R.R. Baxter and Thomas Buergenthal, *Legal Aspects of the Geneva Protocol of 1925: the Control of Chemical and Biological Weapons,* (1971), p.18. A more obvious recent example is the conflict in the former Yugoslavia, which generated extensive legal dispute, both before the International Tribunal for the Former Yugoslavia in the *Tadic* case, and before the International Court of Justice, concerning the nature of the conflict and the standards which should therefore apply.

[6] "Grave breaches" are defined in the Convention for the Amelioration of the Condition of the Wounded and Sick in Armed Forced in the Field (Geneva Convention I), Aug. 12, 1949, Chapter IX, Article 50; Convention for the Amelioration of the Condition of Wounded, Sick and Shipwrecked Members of Armed Forces at Sea (Geneva Convention II), August 12, 1949, Chapter VIII, Article 51; Convention Relative to the Treatment of Prisoners of War (Geneva Convention III), August 12, 1949, Chapter VI, Article 130; Convention Relative to the Protection of Civilian Persons in Times of War (Geneva Convention IV), August 12, 1949, Part IV, Article 147. (Collectively, the "Geneva Conventions"). Additional grave breaches to Protocol I are defined in Articles 11(4) and 85 of that treaty. Article 85 states that "the provisions of the [Geneva] Conventions relating to the repression of breaches and grave breaches, supplemented by this Section, shall apply to the repression of breaches and grave breaches of this Protocol."

[7] The scope and sources of this responsibility, particularly in internal conflicts, are discussed below.

[8] "*Prosecutor v. Dusko Tadic*, a/k/a "Dule" Decision on Interlocutory Appeal, IT-94-1-AR72, October 2, 1995," cited in *International Legal Materials*, vol.35, no.1, (1996) p.71, hereinafter *Tadic*.

of international concern and threats to international peace,[9] have specifically called for those who violate humanitarian law in these contexts to be held accountable.[10] Moreover, recent legal developments serve to bolster the view that there is increasing recognition that fundamental humanitarian standards apply in internal, as in international, conflicts.[11]

Fundamental legal principles

Decisions as to the scope of the Court's jurisdiction should be governed by the fundamental legal principles underlying humanitarian law. Regard should be had to the three fundamental dimensions of humanitarian law, identified by the Appeals Chamber of the ICTY in the *Tadic* case as giving rise to criminal liability in both internal as well as international conflicts: (I) serious violations of Common Article 3 to the Geneva Conventions;[12] (ii) serious violations of general norms on the

---

[9] See Security Council Resolution 864 (1993), concerning the Angolan conflict; Security Council Resolution 788 (1992) concerning the Liberian conflict; Security Council Resolution 733 (1992) concerning Somalia; Security Council Resolution 841 (1993) concerning Haiti; Security Council Resolution (1997) concerning the coup in Sierra Leone.

[10] The Security Council expressly called for individuals to be held accountable for humanitarian law violations in two situations of clearly internal conflict: Security Council Resolution 1072 (1996) on Burundi, and Security Council Resolution 814 (1993) on Somalia. In the former it "recall[ed] that all persons who commit or authorize the commission of serious violations of international humanitarian law are individually responsible for such violations and should be held accountable." Similarly, in relation to Somalia, the Council "[r]eiterate[d] its demand that all Somali parties, including movements and factions, immediately cease and desist from all breaches of international humanitarian law, and reaffirm[ed] that those responsible for such acts were to be held individually accountable...." It also issued such a call in Bosnia at a time when the "international" dimension to the conflict was virtually non-existent, Security Council Resolution 941 (1994).

[11] See, for example, resolution 1998/29 of the United Nations Commission on Human Rights on minimum humanitarian standards (cited above) and its call for a subsequent submission of a report setting out the "Fundamental standards of humanity" at its fifty-fifth session.

[12] Article 3 of the statute of the International Criminal Tribunal for the former Yugoslavia provides as follows:
The International Tribunal shall have the power to prosecute persons violating the laws or customs of war. Such violations shall include, but not be limited to:

protection of victims of internal armed conflict; and (iii) breaches of norms regarding methods and means of warfare.[13]

The first of these, Common Article 3 of the Geneva Conventions, embodies the "elementary considerations of humanity" that constitute the most basic rule of customary international law in all forms of armed conflict.[14] The second, the principle of protection of victims of internal conflicts, is reflected in many provisions of Protocol II Additional to the Geneva Conventions,[15] which "can now be regarded as declaratory of existing rules or as having crystallized emerging rules of customary international law."[16] Thirdly, "breaches of certain fundamental principles and rules regarding methods and means of warfare"[17] also reflect the norm of humane treatment that underlies the universally accepted proposition that

---

(a) employment of poisonous weapons or other weapons calculated to cause unnecessary suffering;
(b) wanton destruction of cities, towns or villages, or devastation not justified by military necessity;
(c) attack, or bombardment, by whatever means, of undefended towns, villages, dwellings, or buildings;
(d) seizure of, destruction or wilful damage done to institutions dedicated to religion, charity and education, the arts and sciences, historic monuments and works of art and science;
(e) plunder of public or private property.

[13] *Tadic.* The Appeals Chamber concluded, having considered relevant *opinio juris* and the internal logic of humanitarian norms, that "all of these factors confirm that customary international law imposes criminal liability for serious violations of Common Article 3, as supplemented by other general principles and rules on the protection of victims of internal armed conflict, and for breaching certain fundamental principles and rules regarding means of combat in civil strife."

[14] Both the ICJ and the ICTY have affirmed the view that Common Article 3 states a rule of customary international law. See also *Nicaragua* v. *United States*, and *Tadic*, Decision on Interlocutory Appeal.

[15] Hereinafter "Protocol II".

[16] *Tadic.*

[17] *Tadic.*

the means of warfare cannot be unlimited.[18] This aspect of humanitarian law prohibits inherently indiscriminate means of combat, and requires that the damage inflicted by means of combat or operations must be proportionate to legitimate military objectives.

The principle of humanity, therefore, underlies these three aspects of humanitarian law and is a principle so fundamental that it governs internal and international conflicts alike, even in the absence of specific legislation.[19] As such it should be the guiding standard in the determination of the crimes to come within the Court's jurisdiction. The International Criminal Tribunal for the Former Yugoslavia has held that "the broad logic of humanitarian law," sets out "elementary considerations of humanity" that are "widely recognized as the mandatory minimum for conduct in armed conflicts of any kind."[20]

In the words of one well-respected humanitarian law scholar, "no self-respecting state would challenge the applicability of such principles [of humanity] in internal conflicts."[21] In this spirit we urge delegates to ensure that the Court is empowered to end impunity for the perpetrators of the crimes set out in the list at the following section of this commentary, irrespective of the nature of the conflict in which they were committed.

---

[18] This principle was set out in the 1907 Hague Regulations Respecting the Laws and Customs of War on Land, Article 22; the regulations are widely acknowledged to constitute customary international law. Protocol I Additional to the Geneva Conventions [hereinafter "Protocol I"] also states the principle at Article 35(1): "In any armed conflict, the right of the Parties to the conflict to choose methods or means of warfare is not unlimited."

[19] The preamble to Protocol II provides that "in cases not covered by the law in force, the human person remains under the protection of the principles of humanity and the dictates of the public conscience." The foundation of this principle is the Martens Clause, set out in the preambles to the 1899 and 1907 Hague Conventions on the Laws and Customs of War on Land, and it has since been expressed in Article 1 of Protocol I and in the preamble to the Conventional Weapons Convention.

[20] *Tadic.*

[21] Theodore Meron, *Human Rights and Humanitarian Norms as Customary International Law* (London: Clarendon Press, 1989), p.74.

Customary international law and existing treaties as guiding principles, not limiting factors

Much of the debate on war crimes during Preparatory Committee sessions focused on the controversial question of the scope of customary international law. The mandate of the Diplomatic Conference is not directed at the codification of crimes that have attained the status of customary international law;[22] trying to mold the Court's statute around a consensus as to the current state of customary international law is both unnecessary and counterproductive. Rather, the International Criminal Court is designed to address the most serious international crimes where national jurisdictions fail to do so. Delegates should use principles derived from customary international law as guidance in deciding what are the most serious international crimes,[23] but not as a limiting factor to justify excluding serious crimes from the Court's jurisdiction. The lack of consensus as to what constitutes customary international law should not be invoked as an excuse to preclude the Court's jurisdiction over grave crimes, many of which are either prohibited by the terms of widely ratified treaties, or by the fundamental principle of humanity. This principle is itself an undisputed cornerstone of the customary international law of armed conflicts.

Similarly, while established treaty language should of course be taken into account in the elaboration of the war crimes section of the statute, delegations should not be

---

[22] The resolution establishing the Preparatory Committee stated that it should "draft texts, with a view to preparing a widely acceptable consolidated text of a convention for an international criminal court as a next step towards consideration by a conference of plenipotentiaries." General Assembly Resolution 50/46. The Preparatory Committee's mandate, as affirmed in paragraph 368 of its report, includes dealing with "definition and elements of crimes" and "principles of criminal law and penalties." As stated by the Jamaican delegate during the February 1997 Preparatory Committee, in neither text is there any reference to customary international law or the need to remain within its confines in defining the crimes to come under the Court's jurisdiction.

[23] In so far customary international law is used to guide such decisions, a progressive approach to the scope of this body of law is encouraged, as exemplified by the jurisprudence of the ICTY referred to below, which considered a broad range of state practice and *opinio juris*-- in reaching the view of customary international law set out in the "Fundamental Legal Principles" section above.

restricted by the exact structure and wording of existing treaties.[24] Rather, for a complete view of the current state of international law, account should be taken of fundamental principles[25] and emerging jurisprudence,[26] which may not be apparent from the text of existing treaties. The process underway is itself an historic treaty drafting exercise which should ensure that the Court has broad jurisdiction over serious war crimes.

LIST OF BASIC CRIMES WHICH SHOULD COME WITHIN THE JURISDICTION OF THE COURT FOR INTERNATIONAL OR NON-INTERNATIONAL CONFLICTS

The Court should have jurisdiction over the crimes set out in the following list whether perpetrated in international or internal armed conflict. The crimes listed below are based on existing humanitarian law, reflecting the three groups of principles and rules of customary international law described by the International

---

[24]The ICTY in *Tadic* reiterated the conclusions of the Nuremberg Tribunal that "a finding of individual criminal responsibility is not barred by the absence of treaty provisions on punishment of breaches."

[25] In the Case Concerning Military and Paramilitary Activities in and Against Nicaragua (Nicaragua v. United States), the International Court of Justice ("ICJ") stated that the obligation to ensure respect for the minimum standards of Common Article 3 of the Geneva Conventions derived "from the general principles of humanitarian law to which the Conventions merely give expression," ICJ, vol.14, June 27, 1986. One such principle is that of "humanity," applicable in international or non-international conflict, referred to by the ICJ in both the Nicaragua v. United States case, and in the Corfu Channel case, Merits, I.C.J. Reports 1949, p.22; para.215.

[26]The judgment in the *Tadic* case, for example, provides important guidance as to how fundamental rules of humanitarian law are being interpreted in the contemporary context, which itself contributes to the evolution of that body of law. Furthermore, the sources of international law, as set out at Article 38 of the statute of the International Court of Justice, include "international conventions ... international custom ... the general principles of law accepted by civilized nations... judicial decisions and teachings of the most highly qualified publicists."

Criminal Tribunal for the Former Yugoslavia and referred to above.[27] We have indicated, in relation to each of these crimes, whether it is currently included in the draft statute, and therefore whether the recommendation is to insert or retain existing provisions. Several crimes included in this list, clearly covered by these fundamental principles of humanity, were omitted from the text prior to the December Preparatory Committee.[28] The inclusion of these serious crimes, committed so frequently in internal armed conflicts, is considered fundamental.

While the following list does not purport to be exhaustive of the crimes to come within the jurisdiction of the Court, it is intended to represent the crimes whose inclusion Human Rights Watch considers indispensable to a credible International Criminal Court.

* *Recommendation 1:* **Include as a crime violence against the life, health, physical or mental well-being of persons taking no direct part in hostilities.**

Comment: The prohibition of violence against the life and person of those taking no direct part in hostilities is contained in Common Article 3(1)(a) of the Geneva Conventions, as expanded by Article 75(2)(a) of Protocol I and Article 4(2)(a) of Protocol II to include violence to the "health, physical or mental well-being of persons." The provisions on grave breaches of the Geneva Conventions contain a prohibition on "wilful killing" and "wilfully causing great suffering or serious injury to body or health."

---

[27] That is, (I) serious violations of Common Article 3; (ii) serious violations of general principles and rules on the protection of victims of internal armed conflict; and (iii) breaches of certain fundamental principles and rules regarding methods and means of warfare, as discussed at Section A, Part 1(b), Recommendation 4 of this document.

[28] Four of these crimes have now been included as Option II to section D, namely starvation of civilians, intentionally launching an attack in the knowledge that such attack will cause incidental loss of life or injury to civilians or damage to civilian objects or the environment, attacks against installations containing dangerous forces if such attack may cause the release of dangerous forces and consequent severe losses among the civilian population, and slavery. These crimes must be retained, and Option II incorporated into the body of the text.

The current text's inclusion of such acts as crimes within the Court's jurisdiction, in current sections A[29] and C[30] of Article 5 of the statute, should be supported.

- ***Recommendation 2:* Include as a crime torture, cruel, inhuman or degrading treatment and punishment, and outrages upon personal dignity.**

Comment: This recommendation is based in the "cruel treatment and torture," "outrages upon personal dignity" and "humiliating and degrading treatment" prohibitions of common Article 3(1) of the Geneva Conventions, and of Article 75(2) of Protocol I and Article 4(2) of Protocol II, and the provision of the Geneva Conventions which establishes "torture or inhuman treatment" as a grave breach of the Conventions.

The draft statute includes, in sections A(b) and C(a), provisions covering the carrying out of such acts.

- ***Recommendation 3:* Include as a crime medical experimentation or physical mutilation.**

Comment: Carrying out biological experiments is expressly included as one of the forms of inhuman treatment constituting a grave breach of the Geneva Conventions. It is also addressed in Article 11 of Protocol 1, which prohibits "physical mutilations," "medical or scientific experiments," and "removal of tissue or organ for transplantation" of persons deprived of liberty, even with their consent, unless those acts are justified by the state of health of the person and are consistent with generally accepted medical standards. In the light of the fundamental nature of this crime, and the horrifying frequency with which experimentation was committed during the Second World War, it should be retained within the crimes over which the Court has jurisdiction.

The draft statute includes, in sections A(b), B(h) and D(j), provisions covering the carrying out of such acts.

---

[29] This section deals with grave breaches.

[30] This section deals with violations of Common Article 3.

- ***Recommendation 4:*** **Include as a distinct category rape, sexual slavery, enforced prostitution, and other sexual or gender-based violence, which may concurrently constitute other applicable crimes provided that the constituent elements of those crimes are present.**

Comment: In light of their status in international law and their frequent commission in situations of armed conflict, the ICC statute should include rape, sexual slavery, enforced prostitution, and other sexual or gender violence as a distinct category of war crimes. It is well established that these crimes can constitute grave breaches[31] and other serious violations of the laws and customs of war in both international and internal armed conflicts.[32] The 1949 Geneva Conventions and the Additional Protocols thereto explicitly condemn rape, enforced prostitution, and acts of indecent assault as violations of international humanitarian law. Moreover, additional Protocol II expressly prohibits rape, enforced prostitution,[33] and slavery[34]

---

[31] If the present structure of the section is retained, distinguishing grave breaches from other war crimes, this should be reflected in part A of Article 5.

[32] The International Committee of the Red Cross (ICRC) has indicated that the grave breach of "wilfully causing great suffering or serious injury to body or health" encompasses rape and that the grave breach of "inhuman treatment" should be interpreted in the context of Article 27 of the Geneva Conventions and its specific prohibition against rape. The Commission of Experts established by the Security Council to examine human rights violations committed in the former Yugoslavia has also recognized that grave breaches include rape and other sexual assaults because they constitute "torture or inhuman treatment" and fall within those acts "wilfully causing great suffering or serious injury to body or health." In *Indictment of Gagovic & Others*, Case No. IT-96-23-I (June 26, 1996), the ICTY indicted eight Serbian officials, charging their acts of rape of fourteen Muslim women as grave breaches of the Geneva Conventions and as violations of the laws and customs of war.

Furthermore, the United States, among other states, has definitively classified rape as a grave breach or war crime under customary international law and the Geneva Conventions. The following international jurisprudence and authorities have recognized rape as a form of torture: the International Criminal Tribunals for the former Yugoslavia and Rwanda; the Inter-American Commission on Human Rights; the U.N. Declaration on the Elimination of Violence Against Women; the Inter-American Convention on the Prevention, Punishment and Eradication of Violence Against Women; the U.N. Rapporteur on Torture; and the U.N. Rapporteur on Violence Against Women, Its Causes and Consequences.

[33] Article 2(e).

[34] Article 2(f).

in internal armed conflicts. Similarly, the International Criminal Tribunal for Rwanda (ICTR) statute incorporates rape, enforced prostitution and other forms of indecent assault within the tribunal's jurisdiction, categorizing them as violations of Common Article 3 to the Geneva Conventions and of Protocol II.[35]

The recognition of rape, sexual slavery, enforced prostitution, and other sexual or gender violence as an explicit category of war crimes should not preclude the prosecution of these acts as additional offences when the elements of such offences are satisfied.[36] The commission of rape and other acts of sexual violence can arise in various circumstances and advance several objectives including, inter alia, "ethnic cleansing"; intimidation, humiliation or punishment; or the demonstration of soldiers' domination over civilians.[37] Accordingly, acts of sexual violence can potentially constitute multiple offenses prohibited by the laws and customs of war, such as violence to life; torture or inhuman treatment; wilfully causing great suffering or serious injury to body or health; enslavement; and outrages upon personal dignity. Failure to specify that rape and other crimes of sexual violence can constitute a range of war crimes runs the risk that such crimes will not be appropriately charged.

Given their grave physical and psychological consequences, it is important to distinguish crimes of sexual violence from the category of offenses against personal

---

[35] Article 4(e), ICTR Statute, reprinted in U.N. Doc. SC/5932.

[36] This approach is followed by the International Criminal Tribunals for the former Yugoslavia and Rwanda, which has charged rape and other acts of sexual violence as one or more of the following crimes: grave breaches (torture and wilfully causing great suffering or serious injury to body or health); violation of the laws and customs of war (torture and outrages upon personal dignity); and crimes against humanity (rape, enslavement, torture, and other inhuman acts).

[37] The special rapporteur on the situation of human rights in the Former Yugoslavia, of the Commission on Human Rights, Tadeusz Mazowiecki, highlighted the role of rape both as an attack on the individual victim and as a method of "ethnic cleansing" intended to humiliate, shame, degrade, and terrify the entire ethnic group. Tadeusz Mazowiecki, *Report on the Situation of Human Rights in the Territory of the Former Yugoslavia*, U.N. Doc. A/48/92-S/25341, (1993), Annex, p.57.

dignity.[38] Characterizing acts of rape, sexual slavery, enforced prostitution, and other sexual or gender violence exclusively as attacks on honor or outrages against personal dignity fails to take into account all the dimensions of such crimes and has frequently allowed for their relatively lenient treatment under the law.

The current text of the statute, at Article (p)*bis* of section B and Article (e)*bis* in section D,[39] provides for crimes of sexual and gender violence to be a separate category of war crimes. Such a specific category should be retained in the final text of the statute, for both internal and international armed conflicts. The wording of (e)*bis* and (p)*bis* should make clear that these crimes may concurrently constitute grave breaches or violations of Article 3 and be prosecuted as such. Human Rights Watch favors the express inclusion of rape, sexual slavery,[40] enforced prostitution,

---

[38] The Commission of Experts established to investigate human rights violations in the former Yugoslavia has considered rape and other forms of sexual assault, including sexual mutilation, to constitute crimes of violence of a sexual nature against the person. It further has noted the prohibition of sexual violence by international humanitarian law through its normative provisions which ban violence against the physical integrity of the person.

[39] Article (p)*bis* of part B and (e)*bis* in part D, include the category of "rape, sexual slavery, enforced prostitution, enforced pregnancy, enforced sterilization, and any other form of sexual violence also constituting a serious violation of...." The texts then refer to a "grave breach of the Geneva Conventions" in Article (p)*bis* for international conflicts and "a violation of Article 3 common to the four Geneva Conventions" in Article (e)*bis* for internal conflicts.

[40] Sexual slavery refers to the exercise of control over another person as chattel for the purpose of performing any sexual conduct whatsoever, whether for consideration or not. It is well-accepted that prohibitions against slavery and slave-related practices have achieved the status of customary international law and attained a *jus cogens* character from which no derogation is permitted, even in times of public emergency. Increasingly, international authorities have recognized that specific crimes of sexual violence can violate international norms against slavery. Moreover, the special rapporteur of the U.N. Sub-Commission on the Prevention of Discrimination and the Protection of Minorities ("U.N. Sub-Commission") released an updated report on slavery in 1982, identifying the following acts, among others, as slavery-like practices: the abuse of women as chattels; the sale of women; and dowry killings. Further, the Working Group on Slavery of the U.N. Sub-Commission classified trafficking in women and children for the purpose of exploitation of prostitution as a form of slavery. Similarly, the U.N. Commission on the Status of Women, as well as the Special Rapporteur on the Suppression of the Traffic in Persons and the Exploitation of the Prostitution of Others, have recognized as a form of enslavement the trafficking of women

forced pregnancy (meaning the confinement or restriction of liberty of a woman impregnated as a result of rape with the intent that the pregnancy proceed to term), sexual mutilation, and forced sterilization and "other sexual or gender-based violence" within this category, to ensure inclusion of the full spectrum of relevant crimes.

• **_Recommendation 5:_ Include as a crime the taking of hostages**

Comment: Hostage-taking is prohibited by common Article 3(1)(b) of the Geneva Conventions, Article 75(2)(c) of Protocol I, and Article 4(2)(c) of Protocol II, and customary international law.

The current text before the Diplomatic Conference supports the inclusion of this crime which appears, without square brackets, in both parts A(h) and C(c) of Article 5 of the draft statute.

• **_Recommendation 6:_ Include as a crime slavery and the slave trade in all their forms.**

Comment: Article 4(2)(f) of Protocol II expressly prohibits "slavery and the slave trade in all their forms." The importance of protecting persons from being subject to slavery is reflected in the wide array of human rights instruments, which enshrine freedom from the slavery as a fundamental non-derogable right, applicable in time of war or peace.[41] The prohibition of slavery is considered _jus cogens_.

The reference to slavery which appears in "Option II" at the end of part D, relating to non-international conflicts, should be retained. We do, however, express our concern over the omission of slavery from the sections dealing with international conflicts, where it would be equally applicable. We therefore urge its retention in part D and insertion in part B.

• **_Recommendation 7:_ Include as a crime attacks against the civilian population as such, or individual civilians.**

---

and children for the purpose of sexual exploitation.

[41] See for example the Convention on the Suppression of Slave Trade and Slavery, 1926; the Supplementary Convention on the Abolition of Slavery, the Slave Trade, and Institutions and Practices Similar to Slavery, 1956; the Protocol amending the Slavery Convention, Convention on the Prevention of Traffic in Persons.

Comment: The protection of the civilian population, in international and internal conflicts, is a fundamental objective of humanitarian law. "Making the civilian population the object of attack" is a grave breach of Protocol I, as set out in Article 85(3) of that protocol. Article 13 of Protocol II specifically states that the civilian population shall "not be the object of attack." Art 51(2) of Protocol I echoes this prohibition.

Delegations are urged to ensure that the ICC has jurisdiction over this most basic crime.
In parts B(a) and D(a), the second option of each article would have this most basic crime deleted from those within the jurisdiction of the Court. Prohibiting direct attacks against the civilian population is one of the most fundamental prohibitions of humanitarian law; as such, the first option of part D(a) and part B(a), which provides for the retention of this crime, should be insisted upon.

- *Recommendation 8:* **Include as a crime attacks against civilian objects.**

Comment: Attacks against civilian objects, being attacks against "all objects which are not military objects," are prohibited by Article 52(1) of Protocol I. It is a basic principle of humanitarian law that civilian and military objectives shall be distinguished, and attacks affecting the civilian population not justified by military necessity shall not be carried out.

The crime included in part B(a)bis should be reflected in part D.

- *Recommendation 9:* **Include as a crime carrying out of attacks which may cause incidental loss of life or injury to civilians or damage to civilians objects, which would be excessive in relation to the concrete and direct military advantage anticipated.**

Comment: Article 57(2) of Protocol 1 obliges parties to "refrain from deciding to launch any attack which may be expected to cause incidental loss of life, injury to civilians, damage to civilian objects, or a combination thereof which would be excessive in relation to the concrete and direct military advantage anticipated."

There is a duty to protect the civilian population, enshrined in international humanitarian instruments.[42] This involves not simply not directing attacks against civilians but also protecting them from the injurious affect of attacks against military objectives but which result in severe civilian losses, disproportionate to the direct military advantage which prompted the attack. Exposing civilians to grave danger by launching attacks which may cause incidental loss or injury is a violation of principle of humanity.

We note that Option II of part D includes "intentionally launching an attack in the knowledge that such attack will cause incidental loss of life or injury to civilians or damage to civilian objects ... or widespread or severe damage to the natural environment," reflecting the comparable provision in part B(b). The addition of this provision which, together with the other articles in Option II, represents a significant improvement in the text, should be supported. The language should however, in line with Article 57(2), cover *wilful* (including reckless) carrying out of such attacks which *may* cause incidental loss of life etc, rather than only those attacks "intentionally" carried out "in the knowledge" of the losses or damage that would ensue.

- **Recommendation 10: Include as a crime the launching of an indiscriminate attack affecting civilians or civilian objects in the knowledge of the excessive loss of life, injury to civilians or damage to civilian objects that would result from the attack.**

Comment: Article 85(3)(b) of Protocol I lists "launching an indiscriminate attack affecting the civilian population or civilian objects in the knowledge that such attack will cause excessive loss of life, injury to civilians or damage to civilian objects..." as one of the acts which, when committed wilfully and causing death or serious injury, constitute a grave breach of Protocol I. Knowingly exposing civilians to grave danger by launching indiscriminate attacks is a flagrant violation of the duty to protect the civilian population, in clear contravention of the principle of humanity.

Indiscriminate attacks which expose the population to serious risk are grave crimes, and should be included within the Court's jurisdiction whether committed in international or non-international conflict.

---

[42]Article 13 of Protocol II and Article 51(1) of Protocol I establish that "the civilian population and individual civilians shall enjoy general protection against the dangers arising from military operations."

- ***Recommendation 11:* Include as a crime attacks against works or installations containing dangerous forces, where such an attack may cause the release of dangerous forces and consequent severe losses among the civilian population, which would be excessive in relation to the concrete and direct military advantage anticipated.**

Comment: Article 56(1) of Protocol I and Article 15 of Protocol II expressly prohibit "attacks against installations containing dangerous forces even where the objects are military objectives, if such attack *may* cause severe losses among the civilian population" (emphasis added). Moreover, Article 85(3) of Protocol I provides that such attacks carried out in the knowledge of the excessive loss of life, injury or damage is a grave breach of that Protocol.

The principles applicable to the protection of civilians from being the object of attack or affected by indiscriminate attacks, and arguments set out in those contexts above, apply equally to these attacks, which by their nature expose the civilian population to very serious danger.

Option II of part D contains a comparable provision to that in part B(b)*bis* Option 1, and the retention of this crime in both types of conflict situation should be supported. The language should however, in line with Article 57(2), cover the *wilful* carrying out of such attacks which *may* cause the relevant loss, injury or damage, rather than only those "intentionally" carried out "in the knowledge" of the losses or damage that would ensue.

- ***Recommendation 12:* Include as a crime the use of weapons, projectiles and material and methods of warfare of a nature to cause excessive injury or unnecessary suffering, or which are inherently indiscriminate.**

Comment: The infliction of unnecessary suffering is clearly prohibited by the principles of humanity.[43] The 1907 Hague Regulations on Land Warfare in Article 23(e) established a categorical prohibition on the employment of "arms, projectiles or material calculated to cause unnecessary suffering." This principle is repeated with slight variation in Article 35(2) of Protocol I to the Geneva Conventions: "It

---

[43] Theodore Meron, *Human Rights and Humanitarian Norms as Customary International Law,* has noted that the prohibition of "means and methods of warfare that cause unnecessary suffering can and should be regarded as [a] necessary and proper derivation from the principle of humanity."

is prohibited to employ weapons, projectiles and material and methods of warfare of a nature to cause superfluous injury or unnecessary suffering." The jurisdiction of the ICC should, in this respect, reflect that of the International Criminal Tribunal for the Former Yugoslavia, which has explicit jurisdiction over the "employment of poisonous or other weapons calculated to cause unnecessary suffering."

Humanitarian law requires that attacks should only be against legitimate military objectives. The employment of weapons which by their inherently indiscriminate nature are incapable of being directed against specific targets should also come within the jurisdiction of the Court, as proposed in Option 3 of part B(o) of Article 5 of the draft statute.

This crime should be included within the jurisdiction of the Court whether committed in international or non-international conflicts. The statute should not exhaustively enumerate the prohibited weapons, as represented (currently under part B(o) of Article 5) as Option 1 or the first part of Option 4. Rather, a definition such as that in Option 3,[44] or the second part of Option 4,[45] which allows the Court the necessary flexibility to accommodate new weapons systems that may develop in the future and changes in the relevant law,[46] should be supported.

- *Recommendation 13:* **Include as a crime pillage and the extensive and wanton destruction of property not justified by military necessity.**

Comment: The "wanton destruction of cities, towns or villages, or devastation not justified by military necessity" and the "plunder of public or private property" are two of the five categories of violations of laws and customs of war specified in

---

[44] "The use of weapons, projectiles and material and methods of warfare of a nature to cause excessive injury or unnecessary suffering, or which are inherently indiscriminate."

[45] Option 4 provides for "weapons, projectiles and material and methods of warfare of a nature to cause excessive injury or unnecessary suffering, or which are inherently indiscriminate, such as but not limited to...."

[46] For example, blinding laser weapons were characterized by the ICRC as an "abhorrent new weapon." They were prohibited by the Protocol on Blinding Laser Weapons to the 1981 Conventional Weapons Convention, quoted in Carnahan & Robertson, "The Protocol on Blinding Laser Weapons," *American Journal of International Law*, vol.90, p.484. The ICC should be able to exercise jurisdiction over such weapons where they violate the aforementioned principles of international law.

Article 3 of the ICTY. These crimes should come within the jurisdiction of the ICC. This conduct constitutes a grave breach of the Geneva Conventions.[47] The Security Council has condemned "the burning of houses, looting of property, and killings of civilians" as "serious violations of international humanitarian law and of human rights."[48] Delegates should support the proposals to include pillage, as prohibited in Article 4(2)(g) of Protocol II, and extensive destruction of property.

Accordingly, the inclusion of this crime in parts B(n) and D(b) should be supported.

• **Recommendation 14: Include as a crime attacks directed against historic monuments, works of art or places of worship that constitute part of the cultural or spiritual heritage of people.**

Comment: The protection of cultural property is a fundamental rule of international humanitarian law and one which the Appeals Chamber of the ICTY in the *Tadic* case described as having attained the status of customary international law.[49] Article 16 of Protocol II contains an express prohibition on directing hostilities against any such objects and using them in support of the military effort. Delegates should support the inclusion in parts B(g) and D(c) of the crime of targeting of such property as a crime whether committed in internal or international conflict.

• **Recommendation 15: Include starvation of civilians as a crime.**

---

[47] Article 50, Chapter XI of the Convention for the Amelioration of the Condition of the Wounded and Sick in Armed Forced in the Field (Geneva Convention I), August 12, 1949, includes the "extensive destruction of property...not justified by military necessity and carried out unlawfully and wantonly." See also Additional Protocol I, Article 85(2).

[48] Note also Security Council Resolution 1019 (1995) which begins: "Deeply concerned at reports, including by UNCRO and United Nations humanitarian agencies, of serious violations of international humanitarian law and of human rights in the former sectors West, North, and South, in the Republic of Croatia, including burning of houses, looting of property, and killings of civilians...."

[49] Setting out its understanding of "the emergence of international rules governing internal strife...," the Appellate Chamber stated that "some treaty rules have gradually become part of customary law. This holds true for common Article 3....but also applies to Article 19 of the Hague Convention for the Protection of Cultural Property in the Event of Armed Conflict of 14 May 1954 and...to the core of Additional Protocol II of 1977." *Tadic* (1996), pp.62-67.

Comment: Article 14 of Protocol II and Article 54 of Protocol I expressly provide that "starvation as a method of combat is prohibited." To this end, they prohibit parties to a conflict from attacking, destroying, removing or rendering useless, for that purpose, objects indispensable to the survival of the civilian population. The fundamental principle of humanity, set out in the context of attacking or exposing to danger the civilian population, is unquestionably applicable to the starvation of that population.

Starvation appears in part B(s), with respect to international conflicts, without brackets, and in part D, as an option (II). Starvation should be criminalized in either type of conflict and, accordingly, delegates should retain Option II in part D.

- **Recommendation 16:** **Include as a crime attacks against non-defended localities and demilitarized zones.**

Comment: Articles 59 and 60 of Protocol I attacks against non-defended localities and the extension of military operations into demilitarized zones, respectively. Furthermore, the "attack or bombardment by whatever means of undefended towns, villages, dwellings or buildings" is specified as one of the crimes within the jurisdiction of the International Criminal Tribunal for the Former Yugoslavia. These are clearly not legitimate military objectives, and the attack of such targets is prohibited by the requirement to protect the civilian population and not to commit violence or attacks against persons taking no active part in hostilities, embodied in Common Article 3 and the principle of humanity.

This crime is not included in the current text with respect to non-international armed conflicts and should be inserted.

- **Recommendation 17:** **Include as a crime attacks against buildings, materials, medical units, transport and personnel entitled to use, in conformity with international humanitarian law, the distinctive emblem of the red cross or red crescent.**

Comment: Article 12 of Protocol II to the Geneva Conventions states that the distinctive emblem shall be "respected in all circumstances," and Article 38 of Protocol I that "it is prohibited to make improper use of the distinctive emblem."

Comparable provisions in the statute at parts B(r) and D(b) should be retained.

- ***Recommendation 18:*** **Include as a crime forcing or compelling persons under the age of eighteen to participate in hostilities.**

Comment: The current text of the statute, at Article (t) of part B and Article (f) of part C, appropriately provides for crimes involving the participation of children under the age of fifteen in armed conflict. However, the options presented fail to recognize the clear emergence of higher standards which seek to exclude children under the age of eighteen from participation in hostilities.[50]

One of the most alarming trends in contemporary armed conflicts is the reliance on children as soldiers.[51] Children are often sought because they are uniquely susceptible to psychological and physical manipulation.[52] In hostilities, their inexperience and immaturity make children particularly vulnerable to trauma, injury, and death.

While the Convention on the Rights of the Child and Protocols I and II to the Geneva Conventions set the minimum age for children's participation in armed conflict at fifteen years,[53] this age is widely acknowledged to be too low and is

---

[50] Among the existing options, all geared to age fifteen, we prefer Option 2 (and its footnote) over the others, with one strong qualification -- we urge that the word "actively" be removed from the option. The detailed footnote attached to the option clearly identifies the types of conduct that would be covered by the definition. Thus the inclusion of the qualifying word "actively" serves no purpose other than to confuse and weaken the text.

Option 2 of parts B and C proposes the following as a war crime: recruiting children under the age of fifteen years into armed forces (section C: or groups) or using them to participate actively in hostilities. The option is followed by a lengthy footnote elaborating on what "using" and "participate" in hostilities mean.

[51] Throughout the world today, an estimated quarter of a million children under the age of eighteen may be serving in government armed forces or armed opposition groups. Rachel Brett and Margaret McCallin, *Children: the Invisible Soldiers*, (Sweden: Radda Barnen, 1996), p. 23.

[52] See generally, "Report of Graca Machel, Expert of the Secretary-General of the United Nations, on the impact of armed conflict on children," A/51/306, paras.34-62, hereinafter "Machel Study".

[53] Convention on the Rights of the Child, Article 38; Additional Protocol I to the Geneva Conventions of 1949, Article 77; and Additional Protocol II to the Geneva Conventions of 1949, Article 4(3).

inconsistent with other international standards. The age at which an individual is liable to be conscripted for military service is eighteen years or higher for nearly all states; the same is true for voting age, the age of political majority,[54] and international standards prohibiting the application of the death penalty to persons under the age of eighteen.[55] Finally, an international consensus is emerging towards establishing eighteen as the age below which persons may neither be recruited nor allowed to participate in hostilities.[56]

---

[54] Seven out of 185 states surveyed indicated a minimum conscription age below eighteen years. Guy Goodwin-Gill and Ilene Cohn, *Child Soldiers: the Role of Children in Armed Conflicts*, (USA: Clarendon Press, 1993), p.8; and ibid, p.197. Six of the 185 states surveyed indicated a voting age lower than eighteen years.

ILO Convention No.138 on Minimum Age also sets eighteen years as the minimum age for admission to employment that is hazardous to the health, safety or morals of young persons. The ILO has suggested that the terms of Convention No.138 may be applied as a corollary to the involvement of children in armed conflicts. See Brett and McCallin, *Children: the Invisible Soldiers*, p. 196.

[55] Convention on the Rights of the Child, Art. 37(a); ICCPR, Article 6(5); Additional Protocol I to the Geneva Conventions, Article 77(5); Additional Protocol II to the Geneva Conventions, Article 6(4).

[56] In 1994 the U.N. Commission on Human Rights convened a working group to draft an optional protocol to the Convention on the Rights of the Child, to raise the minimum age for participation in hostilities and recruitment from fifteen to eighteen. Much progress has been made towards achieving those goals. Already within the U.N. working group, unanimous consensus has been reached on setting the minimum age for compulsory recruitment into government armed forces at eighteen.

A resolution of the 26th International Conference of the Red Cross and Red Crescent (Geneva, December 1995) supports the drafting of the optional protocol and recommended "that parties to conflict refrain from arming children under the age of 18 years and take every feasible step to ensure that children under the age of 18 years do not take part in hostilities." The resolution was adopted by consensus at a meeting open to all states parties to the Geneva Conventions and the Additional Protocols and to representatives of all national societies of the Red Cross and Red Crescent Movement. See Brett and McCallin, *Children: the Invisible Soldiers*, p. 194.

Article 22 of the African Charter on the Rights and Welfare of the Child already provides that state parties shall take all necessary measures to ensure that no child, defined as anyone below the age of eighteen, take part in hostilities and refrain from recruiting any child. OAU Doc. CAB/LEG/24.9/49 (1990).

While recruiting under-eighteens or allowing them to participate in hostilities may not be a sufficiently serious violation of international standards to warrant its inclusion as a crime before this Court, forcing or compelling under-eighteens to participate in hostilities should be included as a war crime.[57]

Forced participation in hostilities would cover children's forced performance of support functions linked to combat such as scouting, manning check points, serving as porters or messengers connected to front line activities, and other activities that expose children to the risks of harm associated with combat. Forced participation in hostilities may also involve forced participation in acts of extreme violence against others, sometimes directed against a child's own family members and community, to break the ties to the community and desensitize the child to death and bloodshed.[58]

In order to end the gross exploitation and abuse of children in armed conflict, it is essential that at least this most extreme form of children's participation in armed conflict, their forced participation in hostilities, be defined as a war crime for all children, not just those under fifteen years of age.

- *Recommendation 19:* **Include as a crime the passing of sentences and the carrying out of executions without previous judgment pronounced by a regularly constituted court, affording all the judicial guarantees which are recognized as indispensable by civilized peoples.**

---

[57] The U.N. expert on the impact of armed conflict on children, Graca Machel, recommended that governments establish legal remedies and institutions that are sufficiently strong to tackle the practice of forced recruitment of children, and thereby also the forced participation of children in hostilities. See Machel Study, para.58. The International Criminal Court should play a critical role in this effort.

Included in the Cape Town Principles of Best Practice and in the Cape Town Plan of Action, drafted in 1997, was a proposal for the establishment of a permanent international criminal court with jurisdiction over the illegal recruitment of children. 1997 Symposium on the Prevention of Recruitment of Children in the Armed Forces and Demobilization and Social Reintegration of Child Soldiers in Africa.

[58] There is evidence from Afghanistan, Mozambique, Colombia, and Nicaragua of child soldiers having been forced to commit atrocities against their families and communities, and in the case of Uganda, to participate in the killing of child recruits who offer resistance to their commanders. Machel Study, para.48; Human Rights Watch, *The Scars of Death: Children Abducted by the Lord's Resistance Army in Uganda* (New York: Human Rights Watch, 1997) pp. 17-18.

Comment: The prohibition on passing sentences in these circumstances is contained in common Article 3(1)(d) of the Geneva Conventions. Article 6 of Protocol II also sets out in some detail "the essential guarantees of independence and impartiality," embodying the right to a fair hearing,[59] as does Article 75(4) of Protocol I. Delegates should support the current inclusion of these crimes in sections A and C of the current text without square brackets.

- *Recommendation 20:* **Include as a crime the imposition of collective punishments.**

Comment: Collective punishments are expressly prohibited by Article 75(2)(d) of Protocol I and Article 4(2)(b) of Protocol II. They violate the principle of personal responsibility.

Human Rights Watch is concerned by the non-inclusion of this crime in the current draft in respect of either international nor non-international conflicts.[60] We therefore urge delegates to include the imposition of collective punishments within the Court's jurisdiction for international and non-international conflicts.

- *Recommendation 21:* **Include as a crime wilfully causing widespread, severe damage to the natural environment.**

Comment: Article 35(3) of Protocol I provides that "it is prohibited to employ methods or means of warfare which are intended, or may be expected, to cause widespread, long-term and severe damage to the natural environment." Article 55 of Protocol I expands upon this prohibition and also states that "care shall be taken in warfare to protect the natural environment against widespread, long term and severe damage." This principle has been codified in substantial detail in other

---

[59] Article 6 reflects the terms of the non-derogable right to a fair trial contained in human rights conventions, such as Article 14 of the International Covenant on Civil and Political Rights.

[60] Prior to the December 1997 Preparatory Committee this crime was included in the compilation of proposals with respect to international conflicts.

international instruments, testifying to the importance attached by the international community to long-term damage to the environment.[61]

- **Recommendation 22:** **Include as a crime terrorism of the civilian population.**

Comment: In addition to attacks against the civilian population as such, or individual civilians, the ICC should have jurisdiction over acts of terrorism within the context of war crimes. Geneva Convention IV states that "all measures of intimidation or of terrorism are prohibited."[62] This is confirmed for non-international conflicts by Article 4(2)(d) of Protocol II. Furthermore, Article 4(d) of the statute of the International Tribunal for Rwanda gives that Tribunal jurisdiction over acts of terrorism.

This crime should be inserted in the war crimes section of the draft statute.

- **Recommendation 23:** **Include as a crime declaring that there will be no survivors, either by express or implicit means.**

Comment: Article 4 of Protocol II, dealing with the "fundamental guarantees," provides expressly that "it is prohibited to declare that there shall be no survivors," as does Article 40 of Protocol I. Delegates should support the inclusion of the crime of declaring that there shall be no survivors in the current text of the statute at part B(j) and B(I).

- **Recommendation 24:** **Include as a crime the forced movement of the civilian population for reasons related to the conflict, unless the security of the civilians involved or imperative military reasons so demand.**

---

[61] The 1977 Convention on the Prohibition of Military or Any Other Hostile Use of Environmental Modification Techniques; the 1982 World Charter for Nature; the Rio Declaration of the 1992 United Nations Conference on Environment and Development; U.N. General Assembly G.A. Res. 47/37 (1992).

[62] Geneva Convention Relative to the Protection of Civilian Persons in Times of War (Geneva Convention IV), August 12, 1949, Article 33. See also Protocol I, Article 51(2), "acts or threats of violence the primary purpose of which is to spread terror among the civilian population are prohibited."

Comment: Displacement causes maximum disruption to the lives of the civilian population and can have the effect of exposing it to great risk, in contravention of the clear obligation to protect the civilian population from dangers arising from military operations. The fundamental nature of the right not to be forcibly moved within a country, or from one country to another, is reflected in the plethora of Security Council Resolutions[63] in recent years testifying to the importance the international community attributes to the voluntary return of refugees and displaced persons.

This crime should be included within the jurisdiction of the ICC. In the context of part B(f) relating to international conflicts, there is an option to have no such provision. At part B(g) it appears unbracketed. We urge the retention of this crime in respect of both classes of conflict, as it embodies a fundamental protection of the civilian population. We further support the wording of B(g) which provides that the only military reasons which might justify displacement of the civilian population are those deemed "imperative"so as to limit the otherwise potentially wide-ranging military reasons which might be invoked for civilian displacement. This reflects the wording of Article 17 of Protocol II.

•   *Recommendation 25*: **Include the crime of perfidy.**

Comment: The commission of perfidy involves inviting the confidence of adversaries by feigning protected status, for example by purporting to be a civilian or non-combatant, wounded or sick person, or bearing a sign, emblems or uniform of the U.N. or other non-parties to conflict, or by use of flag of truce or surrender.[64] To do so inevitably undermines the force of humanitarian law and ultimately jeopardizes the protection it seeks to afford to these categories of persons. Delegations should therefore support the inclusion of this crime within the Court's jurisdiction, currently excluded in respect of both international or non-international conflicts.

•   *Recommendation 26*: **Include utilizing the presence of a civilian or other protected person to render certain points, areas, or military**

---

[63] See, for example, Security Council Resolution 811 (1993), Security Council Resolution 941 (1994), Security Council Resolution 1001 (1995), Security Council Resolution 1036 (1996), and Security Council Resolution 1076 (1996).

[64] Article 37 of Additional Protocol I.

forces which otherwise would be legitimate military objectives, immune from military operations.

Comment: The principles underlying the criminality of perfidy apply also to the use of civilians and other protected groups as human shields. It is an abuse of the principles of humanitarian law for military gain, and as such ultimately undermines the ability of that body of law to afford the relevant groups the necessary protection. In exposing noncombatants to attacks, it is prohibited by the most basic principles of the laws of war.

Delegations should therefore supports the inclusion of this crime within the Court's jurisdiction, as in part B(q) in respect of international conflicts.[65] However, that since the principle that the civilian population be protected is equally applicable in non-international conflict, this crime should extend to this type of conflict also.

OTHER CRIMES UNDER CUSTOMARY INTERNATIONAL LAW

- *Recommendation:* **Insert a sub-section indicating that nothing in the enumeration of war crimes in Article 5 should prevent the Court from exercising jurisdiction with respect to other crimes which have attained the status of customary international law.**[66]

Comment: The Appeals Chamber of the International Criminal Tribunal for the Former Yugoslavia stated in the Tadic case the following:
"[T]hree Member States of the Council, namely France, the United States and the United Kingdom, expressly stated that Article 3 of the statute also covers obligations stemming from agreements in force between the conflicting parties, that is Article 3 common to the Geneva Conventions and the two additional Protocols... In other words, Article 3 [of the Tribunal's statute] functions as a residual clause designed to ensure that no serious violation of international humanitarian law is taken away from the jurisdiction of the International Tribunal. [It] aims to make such jurisdiction watertight and inescapable ....Thus, if correctly interpreted,

---

[65] See the proposal of the delegation of the United States.

[66] Note that this recommendation should not be seen to imply that those crimes enumerated in the statute itself need have attained the status of customary international law, but only that this limitation be imposed on the flexibility of the Court to include within its jurisdiction crimes beyond those mentioned in Article 5.

Article 3 fully realizes the primary purpose of the establishment of the International Tribunal, that is, not to leave unpunished any person guilty of any such serious violation, whatever the context within which it may have been committed.[67]

A similar provision should be included for the ICC. The provision should, of course, extend only to customary international law that exists at the time of the commission of the crime in question, and as such would not raise any questions as to the retroactivity. Moreover, this would ensure the flexibility that the Court will need to respond to the emergence of new crimes and the development of customary international law in the future.

THE THRESHOLD

• *Recommendation:* **The Court's jurisdiction over war crimes should not be restricted to crimes committed as part of a systematic plan or policy, or as part of the large-scale commission of such crimes.[68] The first of the three options, which would limit the Court's jurisdiction to crimes committed in this context, should be deleted. While either the second or third option is acceptable, the third is preferable.**

Comment: The proposition that the ICC should try only egregious violations of humanitarian law should be supported. We suggest that this is reflected in the statement of the preamble which makes clear that the Court "is intended to exercise jurisdiction only over the most serious crimes of concern to the international community as a whole." We support the ability of the prosecutor to prioritize and to chose to pursue the more serious over the less serious crimes, and the duty of the Court to take into account the gravity of the crime in determining sentence.[69] The existence of a plan or policy, and the massive nature of crimes, would undoubtedly be factors relevant to such determinations.

However, we oppose restricting the Court's jurisdiction to crimes committed in these circumstances. To say a crime is "egregious" is not synonymous with saying it was committed on a massive scale or in the context of a plan or policy: there are

---

[67] *Tadic*, p.61.

[68] See the proposal of the United States as incorporated in the consolidated text.

[69] See in this respect the section of the full report in relation to Penalties.

circumstances in which certain terrible acts of torture or mutilation, for example, carried out other than pursuant to a "policy," would nonetheless constitute very serious crimes.

It should be borne in mind in this context that the ICC will not prosecute states, but individuals. As such, the existence of a "plan or policy" is, in our view, an inappropriate prerequisite to the Court's assuming jurisdiction and rendering individual justice. There is no justification to assert that no forum should be available to try individuals who carry out atrocities of their own volition, as opposed to those who carry out the same acts pursuant to orders to do so.[70]

Even in cases where there was in fact such a plan or policy, it may not be possible in the particular case to obtain sufficient evidence to prove its existence. The Court must not be prevented from investigating and prosecuting serious crimes where there is clear evidence of their commission but insufficient evidence as to the plan or policy which lay behind their execution.

The language of the first option, restricting jurisdiction to acts "committed as part of a systematic plan or policy or part of a large-scale commission of such crimes," is borrowed virtually wholesale from the definition of crimes against humanity.[71] There is no legal support for imposing this additional element of proof in the case of war crimes.[72] Setting the threshold at such a high level will result in a definition of such crimes that is substantially narrower than that contained in the definitions of grave breaches of the Geneva Conventions of 1949 and the terms of Common Article 3 to the Conventions. As a result, if this language were to be adopted for the

---

[70] As stated in the section of the full report, on "Defenses," superior orders should not serve to exonerate anyone from responsibility for crimes within the jurisdiction of the Court. Nor, however, do they create a greater degree of responsibility. It would, in our view, be absurd for the Court only to be able to exercise jurisdiction where a crime committed by individual soldiers was carried out pursuant to centralized plan or policy, but not if there were some different motivation.

[71] The statute of the International Criminal Tribunal for Rwanda, for example, states at Article 3 that the tribunal has jurisdiction over crimes against humanity committed "as part of a widespread or systematic attack."

[72] As Professor Theodore Meron has written: "Proof of systematic and deliberate planning... is not required to establish the violation of Common Article 3 or Additional Protocol II." See Theodore Meron, "International Criminalization of Internal Atrocities," *American Journal of International Law* (1989), pp.554-7.

ICC, the Court's jurisdiction would fall short of covering even those violations for which humanitarian law prescribes an express duty to punish.[73]

The third option, which provides for no threshold, should be supported. The statute currently provides for the prosecutor to take into account the gravity of the alleged offense in determining whether a prosecution is in the interests of justice.[74] We support this, and believe that the existence of a plan or policy would be a factor in such a determination. For this reason, while the second option is entirely acceptable in terms of its substantive effect, we consider it unnecessary. The second option closely shadows the first, with the critical difference that the Court shall have jurisdiction "in particular"-- and not exclusively -- in respect of crimes committed as part of a plan or policy. The reference to the Court having jurisdiction "in particular" where such a plan or policy exists strikes us as peculiar: the court has jurisdiction or it does not. Clearly, it may decide whether or not to exercise that jurisdiction, for example on the basis of the interests of justice, in any particular case. However, subject to the observation that the provision appears superfluous and slightly confusing, we have no strong objection to either Options two or three.

Part 2: CRIMES AGAINST HUMANITY

THE CHAPEAU TO THE DEFINITION

Nexus with armed conflict

• **Recommendation: Delete the option in the chapeau that would require a nexus between crimes against humanity and the existence of armed conflict.**

---

[73] The obligation to impose "effective penal sanctions" is established in the Convention for the Amelioration of the Condition of the Wounded and Sick in Armed Forced in the Field, August 12, 1949, Chapter IX, Article 49; Convention for the Amelioration of the Condition of Wounded, Sick and Shipwrecked Members of Armed Forces at Sea, August 12, 1949, Chapter VIII, Article 50; Convention Relative to the Treatment of Prisoners of War, August 12, 1949, Chapter VI, Article 129; Convention Relative to the Protection of Civilian Persons in Times of War, August 12, 1949, Part IV, Article 146.

[74] Article 54(2)([47(1 *bis)*](b)(ii)*bis*. This reflects the terminology in the preamble.

Comment: It is now well established in international law that crimes against humanity can be committed in time of war or peace. While Article 6(c) of the Nuremberg Charter clearly envisaged crimes against humanity within the jurisdiction of the Nuremberg Tribunals as applying only to acts committed in connection with World War Two, such a nexus has been consistently rejected subsequent to Nuremberg.[75]

The special rapporteur on the Draft Code of Crimes against the Peace and Security of Mankind, stated in 1989 that crimes against humanity are "separate from... war crimes... [N]ot only the 1954 Draft but even conventions which have entered into force (on genocide and apartheid) no longer link that concept to a state of war."[76] Most recently, the work of the ad hoc tribunals for both the former Yugoslavia as well as Rwanda has confirmed that the nexus requirement has become obsolete.[77] Security Council Resolution 808, establishing the International Criminal Tribunal for the Former Yugoslavia (ICTY), contains the observation that crimes against humanity are directed against a civilian population and "are prohibited regardless of whether they are committed in an armed conflict, international or internal in character."[78] The Appellate Chamber of the ICTY in the *Prosecutor v. Tadic* case invoked customary international law when it stated quite clearly that "customary

---

[75] The Appellate Chamber of the International Criminal Tribunal for the Former Yugoslavia (ICTY), in the *Prosecutor* v. *Dusko Tadic* case stated that the nexus between crimes against humanity and crimes against peace or war crimes was "peculiar to the jurisdiction of the Nuremberg Tribunal... there is no logical or legal basis for this requirement and it has been abandoned in subsequent State practice with respect to crimes against humanity." (October 2, 1995) reprinted in *International Legal Materials*, vol.35, p.72 (1996). (Hereinafter, *Tadic.*)

[76] "Draft Code of Crimes against the Peace and Security of Mankind Seventh Report [1989]", *II Yearbook of International Law,* Comm'n 81, 86, U.N. Doc. A/CN.4/419/Add.1.

[77] The statute for the Rwanda Tribunal makes no reference to the existence of an armed conflict as a prerequisite for the commission of such crimes.

[78] Security Council Resolution 808 (1993), U.N. Doc. S/25704/Add.1 reprinted in *International Legal Materials,* vol.32, (1993), p.1173, established the statute of the International Criminal Tribunal for the Former Yugoslavia (hereinafter ICTY Statute).

international law no longer requires any nexus between crimes against humanity and armed conflict..."[79]

It should be noted that while the Nuremberg Charter required that crimes against humanity be committed "*before or during* war [emphasis added]," the current draft contains the formulation "*in* armed conflict [emphasis added]." The retention of this provision in Article 5 would establish a position even more restrictive than that at the time of Nuremberg. This would constitute a seriously retrograde step in international law, entirely inconsistent with developments in international law.

Moreover, and most importantly, such a link would mean that even the gravest of crimes, when committed outside the context of armed conflict, would continue to go unpunished. The gravity of the crimes included within the definition of crimes against humanity demands prosecution of the perpetrators, whatever the context in which these crimes occur. Delegates are therefore urged to ensure that this limitation does not remain in the statute.

The widespread and/or systematic requirement

• **Recommendation: The chapeau to the definition of crimes against humanity should refer to those enumerated acts committed in connection with a widespread *or* systematic (as opposed to widespread *and* systematic) attack on any civilian population. Delete the requirement that the crimes be committed "on a massive scale."**

Comment: Crimes against humanity are among the gravest crimes of concern to the international community as a whole. As such, there can be little argument that the definition should not cover isolated or minor crimes.[80] However, to require that crimes against humanity be committed as part of both a widespread *and* systematic attack imposes too high a threshold and is inconsistent with existing international standards. The same applies to the words "on a massive scale" currently in square

---

[79] *Tadic*, p.72.

[80] See *United States* v. *Josef Altstoetter*, reprinted in *III Trials of War Criminals before the Nuremberg Military Tribunals under Control Council Law*, no.10 954, p.982 (1951) (hereinafter *Justice*) which stated that "isolated cases of atrocity or persecution whether committed by private individuals or governmental authority..." do not constitute crimes against humanity.

brackets in the chapeau, which should be deleted. The requirement that the enumerated acts be committed as part of a widespread *or* systematic attack is consistent with the state of current international law.

The ICTY stated in the *Prosecutor v. Tadic* judgment that "it is now well established that the requirement that the acts be directed against a civilian 'population' can be fulfilled if the acts occur on *either* a widespread basis *or* in a systematic manner."[81] It has gone on to note that "as long as there is a link with the widespread or systematic attack against a civilian population, a single act could qualify as a crime against humanity."[82]

The same approach was taken by the International Law Commission's special rapporteur in the seventh report on the Draft Code of Crimes Against the Peace and Security of Mankind, where he observed that acts constituting crimes against humanity must be *either* mass violations *or* individual acts which are "part of a system or plan."[83]

The proposed limitation on the "grounds" on which crimes against humanity are committed

- *Recommendation*: **The chapeau should not include any reference to the specific grounds on which crimes against humanity are committed.**

Comment: The Nuremberg Charter and Control Council Law No.10, drafted by the Allies immediately subsequent to the Nuremberg Charter and under which the Nuremberg Trials were conducted, divides crimes against humanity into two

---

[81] *International Legal Materials,* p.942.

[82] Prosecutor v. Mile Msksic, Miroslav Radic, and Veselin Sljivancanin, "Review of the Indictment Pursuant to Rule 61 of the Rules of Procedure and Evidence, Case No. IT-95-13-R61, T.Ch. I (3 Apr. 1996)" quoted in *Tadic, International Legal Materials*, vol.36, p.943.

[83] "Draft Code of Crimes Against the Peace and Security of Mankind Seventh Report", Mr. Doudou Thiam, Special Rapporteur, (1989), *II Year Book of International Law Commission*, 81, pp.88-89, U.N. Doc. A/CN.4/419/Add.1

categories: inhumane acts and persecution.[84] Motive is relevant only to the latter,[85] on the basis that "[c]ertain acts are so heinous and destructive of a person's humanity that they *per se* are crimes. Others are crimes because the perpetrator acts against the victim based on political, racial or religious grounds and attacks humanity through some of the most basic groups into which it is organized."[86]

The omission of any specified motive from the definition of crimes against humanity would be consistent with the statute of the International Criminal Tribunal for the Former Yugoslavia (ICTY) which makes grounds for commission relevant only in the case of persecutions, not for any of the enumerated inhumane acts which also constitute crimes against humanity.[87] Commentators have noted that by making this distinction, the Security Council "thus seems to have assumed that customary international law made motive for the non-persecution offenses irrelevant beyond any doubt."[88] Likewise, the 1996 International Law Commission Draft Code eliminates the motive requirement for crimes against humanity generally.[89]

---

[84] Control Council Law No.10, reprinted in *VI Trials of War Criminals before the Nuremberg Military Tribunals under Control Council Law*, No. 10, Article 6(c), XVIII, XIX (1952).

[85] Jaons Ratner and Steven Abrams, *The Criminalization of Atrocities in International Law*, (1997), p. 61.

[86] Ibid. This "basic groups" argument also provides further support for the contention that gender should be included as a category for purposes of defining persecution.

[87] Article 5 of ICTY Statute, p.1173.

[88] Ratner and Abrams, *Criminalization of Atrocities*, p.62 (quoting "Report of the Secretary-General pursuant to paragraph 2 of Security Council Resolution 808 (1993)", May 3, 1993, U.N. Doc. S/25704, p.9).

[89] The Draft Code retains a motive requirement for "persecution" and "institutionalized discrimination" but not for crimes against humanity generally. (*International Law Commission Report*, (1996), pp.93-4, (Article 18).

SPECIFIC ACTS CONSTITUTING CRIMES AGAINST HUMANITY

Enforced disappearance

- **Recommendation:Include enforced disappearance of persons within the jurisdiction of the court.**

Comment: That enforced disappearances constitute crimes against humanity has been recognized by the Organization of American States,[90] the United Nations General Assembly,[91] the European Parliament,[92] as well as in national legislation.[93]

Human Rights Watch is concerned by the footnote to the current text, which expresses uncertainty as to the inclusion of this particular crime against humanity. Reports prepared by this organization attest to the frequency with which "disappearances" have been carried out in recent decades and the profound gravity of the crime, in terms both of the impact on the victim directly and society more broadly. We urge delegates to ensure its inclusion as a crime against humanity within the jurisdiction of the Court.

Persecution

Section 1(h) of the current draft reads:
"persecution against any identifiable group or collectivity on political, racial, national, ethnic, cultural or religious [*or gender*] [or other similar] grounds [and in connection with other crimes within the jurisdiction of the court]."
A footnote after the word "grounds" reads "This also includes, for example, social, economic, and mental or physical disability grounds."

---

[90] Inter-American Convention on the Forced Disappearance of Persons, June 9, 1994, preamble para.6 and OAS General Assembly Resolution 666 (XIII-O/83).

[91] Declaration on the Protection of All Persons from Enforced Disappearance, U.N. GA RES 47/133, adopted December 18, 1992.

[92] Resolution 828/84, Parliamentary Assembly of the Council of Europe.

[93] See 1992 French statute *Nouveau Code Pénal*, Articles 212-1 (Fr.), reprinted in Leila Sadat Wexler, "The Interpretation of the Nuremberg Principles by the French Court of Cassation: From Touvier to Barbie and Back Again," Columbia Journal of Transnational Law, vol. 32, (1994), p.380.

•   ***Recommendation 1:***
    (a) Retain persecution as a separate sub-category of crimes against humanity
and
    (b) delete the reference to "in connection with other crimes within jurisdiction of the Court."

Comment:
(a) Persecution is defined by the ICTY, in the case of the *Prosecutor v. Dusko Tadic* as "some form of discrimination that is intended to be and results in an infringement of an individual's fundamental rights. However, it is the discrimination itself, resulting in the grave violation of human rights, that constitutes the crime."[94] As such it is a serious crime, distinct in nature from the other acts enumerated in Article 5 under the heading "Crimes Against Humanity."

That persecution constitutes a crime against humanity has been well established in international law since crimes against humanity were first defined in the Nuremberg Charter. The Nuremberg Charter,[95] Control Council Law No. 10, the Tokyo Charter,[97] and the statutes of the International Criminal Tribunal for the Former

---

[94] *Tadic,* p.941.

[95] The Charter of the International Military Tribunal Annexed to the London Agreement, 8 August 1945; 8 UN Treaty Series 279; 59 Stat.1544, 8AS No.472. Reprinted in *American Journal of International Law,* vol.39, (1945), p.257.

[96] Control Council Law No.10 defined crimes against humanity as "atrocities and offenses, including but not limited to murder, extermination, enslavement, deportation, imprisonment, torture, rape, or other inhumane acts committed against any civilian population, or persecution on political, racial or religious grounds whether or not in violation of the domestic laws of the country where perpetrated."

[97] Charter of the International Military Tribunal for the Far East, Tokyo, January 19, 1946, Article 5(c). Reprinted in B. Ferencz, *Defining International Aggression,* p.523.

Yugoslavia (ICTY)[98] and the International Criminal Tribunal for Rwanda (ICTR),[99] all define crimes against humanity as including persecution as a separate subcategory of such crimes.

To remove persecution from the definition of crimes against humanity would constitute a retrograde step, as would the inclusion of language setting out specific grounds on which crimes against humanity are committed. The *nota bene* to the proposed chapeau states that if the provision relating to the grounds on which crimes against humanity must be committed is included in the chapeau, the text of sub-paragraph 1(h) should be reconsidered. Persecution should remain on the list of enumerated acts.

(b) Human Rights Watch believes that the requirement that persecution be committed "in connection with other crimes within the jurisdiction of the Court" should be removed. In practice, persecution will often be accompanied by the commission of other inhumane acts, or coupled with the commission of other crimes within the Court's jurisdiction. This is not, however, a requirement for persecution to constitute a crime against humanity.

While Article 6 of the Nuremberg Charter clearly did envisage that persecution would be committed "in execution of or in connection with any crime within the jurisdiction of the Tribunal," international law has developed since Nuremberg to reject that connection. Indeed in Control Council Law No. 10, drafted by the Allies immediately subsequent to the Nuremberg Charter, the above wording was absent and the necessary connection with the commission of other crimes disappeared.[100] Delinking other inhumane acts from persecution is supported by the ICTY in the

---

[98] Article 5(h) of the ICTY Statute.

[99] Article 3(h) of the statute of the International Criminal Tribunal for Rwanda (hereinafter ICTR Statute), created by Security Council Resolution S/RES/955 (1994), adopted by the Security Council at its 3453rd meeting, on November 8, 1994.

[100] Control Council Law No.10, 1952, art. 6(c). See also the *Justice* case (1951) which notes that while the Charter "defines crimes against humanity as inhumane acts, etc., committed 'in execution of, or in connection with, any crime within the jurisdiction of the tribunal,'... in C.C. 10 the words last quoted are deliberately omitted."

parts of the Tadic judgment cited above[101] and by the case of *Fédération Nationale des Deportés et Résistants Internes et Patriotes and Others v. Barbie.*[102] In the *Barbie* case, the court stated that: "it is not necessary to have a separate act of an inhumane nature to constitute persecution; the discrimination itself makes the act inhumane."[103]

Any attempt to link persecution to other crimes in this way distorts the notion of persecution. Limiting the Court's jurisdiction over persecution to circumstances where other crimes have been committed would render meaningless subparagraph (h). Its effect would be to remove the prosecution of persecution per se--a fundamental and long established crime against humanity--from the Court's jurisdiction.

Gender persecution

• **Recommendation 2: If the grounds for persecution are set out in the statute, gender should be included as one such ground.**

Comment: In recent years, there has been increasing legal recognition that gender often constitutes a ground on which persecution is carried out. The ICC, as a forward looking institution charged with prosecuting crimes against humanity in the modern world, should reflect this reality and the corresponding legal developments.

It is in the area of refugee law that the concept of persecution based on gender has been most developed.[104] This was recognized by the Platform for Action and the

---

[101] As set out above, the ICTY made clear that persecution as a crime against humanity is of a nature quite distinct from others: "it is the discrimination itself, resulting in the grave violation of human rights, that constitutes the crime." *Tadic*, 36 *International Legal Materials*, p.956.

[102] Cour de Cassation, Criminal Chamber 1983-85, *International Law Review*, vol.78, (1988), p.124.

[103] Cour de Cassation, ibid, p.143.

[104] Most recently, a United Nations Expert Group Meeting, held in November 1997, concluded that "[a]lthough the term 'gender-based persecution' does not appear within any of the legal instruments, it encompasses the forms of harm that are regularly suffered by women and girls everywhere and which are directed at them because of their sex"

Beijing Declaration which emerged from the Fourth World Conference on Women convened in Beijing in September 1995 which, in the "Women in Armed Conflict" section, expressly raised the issue of gender-based persecution in the context of refugee law.[105]

The Executive Committee of the United Nations High Commissioner for Refugees (hereinafter the UNHCR Executive Committee) has, in a long series of other "conclusions," reinforced the growing trend towards the recognition of gender as one of the bases of persecution. Among those conclusions it has stated that: "In accordance with the principle that women's rights are human rights, these guidelines should recognize as refugees women whose claim to refugee status is based upon well-founded fear of persecution for reasons enumerated in the 1951 Convention and 1967 Protocol, including persecution through sexual violence or other gender-related persecution."[106]

The Convention Relating to the Status of Refugees,[107] on which the UNHCR Executive Committee based many of its conclusions, does not itself expressly include gender as a basis for persecution. This is perhaps unsurprising since the convention was drawn up in 1951, however the persecution of "particular social

---

(para. 20). Furthermore, "as sexual violence in the context of armed conflict contravenes norms of international law, the expert group considered that it meets the definition of "persecution" in international refugee law... [and] recognized that severe discrimination and harassment, particularly, but not exclusively, in armed conflict or in an atmosphere of insecurity may constitute persecution". United Nations Division for the Advancement of Women: "Gender-based persecution - Report of the Expert Group Meeting," held in Toronto, Canada, November 9-12, 1997, EGM/GBP/1997/Report, pp. 40-1.

[105] United Nations Department of Public Information, *Platform for Action and Beijing Declaration* (1996), p. 84.

[106] Executive Committee, Conclusion No.77, "General Conclusion on International Protection," (1995). See also Executive Committee, Conclusion No.73, "Refugee Protection and Sexual Violence," (19XX) and Executive Committee, Conclusion No. 79, "General Conclusion on International Protection," (1996), Executive Committee, Conclusion No. 81, "General Conclusion on International Protection," (1997).

[107] Convention relating to the Status of Refugees, (hereinafter Refugee Convention), 189 UN Treaty Series (1951), p.150.

groups" which are included within the convention has been interpreted as covering persecution based on gender.[108] In this respect, the UNHCR Executive Committee has "[r]ecognized that States, in the exercise of their sovereignty, are free to adopt the interpretation that women asylum-seekers who face harsh or inhuman treatment due to their having transgressed the social mores of the society in which they live may be considered as a 'particular social group' within the meaning of Article 1 (A) (2) of the 1951 Refugee Convention."[109]

The proposal to include persecution on "other similar grounds" in the current text carries a footnote after the word "grounds" which states that this includes, among others, "social" grounds. In light of the aforementioned Executive Committee conclusions, this may incorporate persecution against women. We believe that this does not, however, undermine the importance of an express reference to gender persecution, to reflect developments in this area and to recognize the reality and the gravity of persecution on the grounds of gender.

Persecution on other grounds

• **Recommendation: The definition of persecution should set out in the broadest possible terms the grounds on which persecution might be committed. These grounds should include those specified in the current draft[110] but also sexual orientation, economic grounds, or disability, for example. Finally, the inclusion of a general category covering other grounds not specified in the list, should be strongly supported by delegations.**

Comment: Given the gravity of the crime of persecution, Human Rights Watch believes that the list of grounds of discrimination should be drawn broadly while setting out examples of such groups that have historically suffered persecutions.

---

[108] Determination of refugee status in the convention is based on a finding that an applicant is seeking asylum based on a "well-founded fear of being persecuted for reasons of race, religion, nationality, membership in a particular social group, or political opinion." Refugee Convention, ibid, Article I(A)(2).

[109] UNHCR Executive Committee, Conclusion No.39, "Refugee Women and International Protection", (1985).

[110] As mentioned earlier, the current draft refers to "political, racial, national, ethnic, cultural or religious, [or gender] [or other similar] grounds."

History indicates that groups have been persecuted for a wide range of reasons, going beyond those specified in the current definition of persecution. During the atrocities of the Second World War, for example, people were subjected to extreme forms of persecution, with devastating effects, on the grounds of sexual orientation, property ownership, or disability. This reality should be reflected in the text of the statute. While we note that the footnote to the relevant article states that "other similar grounds" is intended to cover social, economic, mental or physical disability, these categories merit specific reference in the statute. Sexual orientation, which is not reflected anywhere in the current draft, is among those criteria that require incorporation.

A general category referring to "other grounds" would ensure that no group which is singled out and subject to persecution is excluded from the scope of the definition. One commentator has offered a definition of persecution which highlights that persecution may occur "simply because the perpetrator sought to single out a given category of victims for reasons peculiar to the perpetrator."[111] As such the statute should not seek to list exhaustively all possible categories of victims a perpetrator may identify for the purposes of persecution.

We therefore urge that the reference to other grounds be retained, subject to the deletion of the term "similar," which could result in an unacceptably restrictive definition.

---

[111] M. Cherif Bassiouni has defined persecution as: "State action or policy leading to the infliction upon an individual of harassment, torment, oppression, or discriminatory measures, designed to or likely to produce physical or mental suffering or economic harm, because of the victim's beliefs, views, or membership in a given identifiable group (religious, social, ethnic, linguistic etc.), or simply because the perpetrator sought to single out a given category of victims for reasons peculiar to the perpetrator." *Crimes Against Humanity in International Criminal Law*, (Netherlands: Martinus Nijhoff Publishers, 1992), p.317.

SECTION B: THE JURISDICTION OF THE COURT

Introduction
This section addresses Articles 6 (the exercise of jurisdiction), 7 (preconditions to the exercise of jurisdiction), 9 (acceptance of the jurisdiction of the Court) and the "further option" for these articles in the current text of the statute. In Part 1 below, we explain the principles which underlie our position on Articles 6, 7 and 9. We then make our recommendation as to appropriate provisions on jurisdiction, and comment on this recommendation and key proposals contained in the current text (Part 2).

UNDERLYING PRINCIPLES

The satisfactory resolution of the question of the Court's jurisdiction is critical to the success of the ICC initiative. The objective of the Diplomatic Conference must be to create a strong independent and effective international court that can exercise jurisdiction over genocide, crimes against humanity and war crimes, free from political manipulation. A statute which saddles the Court with inherent susceptibility to such manipulation will not yield the sort of justice that the international community urgently demands. Allowing individual states to select the crimes or types of conduct over which they accept the Court's jurisdiction, or worse, to chose on a case-by-case basis when to allow the Court to proceed and when not to, foments selectivity and arbitrariness.

Legitimate state interests are safeguarded elsewhere in the ICC statute.[112] While a state consent regime is therefore unnecessary to meet legitimate interests, such a regime would render the Court vulnerable to the illegitimate interests that recalcitrant states may have in shielding perpetrators of atrocities from the reach of criminal justice. Should the statute provide the framework for states to do so, it would seriously undermine the legitimacy and credibility of the ICC.

---

[112] Legitimate state interests, for example in the prosecution of crimes within its jurisdiction, are more than adequately protected by the firm principle of complementarity enshrined in Article 15[11]. It ensures that, where a state is willing and able to do so, the ICC cannot interfere with its ability to perform its proper domestic judicial function. Note that the ability to challenge admissibility on this basis applies to both state parties and non-state parties. No consent of any state, party or non-party, should be required for the exercise of the Court's jurisdiction.

The ICC should have jurisdiction over the core crimes of genocide, crimes against humanity, and war crimes. The statute should clearly confer on the ICC the power to prosecute these crimes which are "universal in nature, well recognized in international law as serious breaches of international humanitarian law, and transcending the interest of any one State," irrespective of where they were committed or by whom. By ratifying the statute, states would then confer upon the Court the power that each of them would have individually,[113] to investigate and prosecute the crimes subject to universal jurisdiction, without being required to obtain the "acceptance" or "consent" of any State.[114] Any other position would result in an ICC, established with the specific role of administering criminal justice when national systems fail, having less jurisdictional ability to fulfil this mandate than any one of the state parties that collectively created it.[115]

The existence of universal jurisdiction over genocide, crimes against humanity and certain categories of war crimes is well established. Genocide has been acknowledged as subject to universal jurisdiction under customary international law by several commentators[116] and in the *Third Restatement of Foreign Relations Law*

---

[113] The Nuremberg Judgment reasoned that: "The signatory Powers created this Tribunal, defined the law it was to administer, and made regulations for the proper conduct of the Trial. *In doing so, they have done together what any one of them might have done singly....(emphasis added),*" "International Military Tribunal (Nuremberg), Judgment and Sentences," *American Journal of International Law*, vol.41, (1947), p.216.

[114] The ICC will in fact have a mandate that is far more universal in its scope than that of the Nuremberg tribunal; given the number of states involved in creating this historic institution, its permanence and general geographic application, and the crimes covered by it.

[115] See John Dugard, "Obstacles in the Way of An International Criminal Court," *Cambridge Law Journal*, vol.56, no.2, (1997), p.337, where the author points out that state consent would mean that the "court actually has less power to bring to justice the suspect than either the territorial state or the custodial state, each of which could bring the suspect to justice without the consent of any other state." By virtue of universal jurisdiction, this applies also to any other state.

[116] Kenneth C. Randall, "Universal Jurisdiction Under International Law," *Texas Law Review*, vol.66, (1988), p.131.

of the United States.[117] The application of universal jurisdiction to crimes against humanity is similarly well established, and can be seen from the jurisdiction of the Nuremberg tribunal[118] and from subsequent domestic litigation.[119]

That war crimes are "crimes *ex jure gentium* and are thus triable by the Courts of all States"[120] has also been widely recognized.[121]   The Geneva Conventions

---

[117] *Restatement of the Law (Third), Foreign Relations of the United States,* (American Law Institute, 1987), para.404: "Universal jurisdiction to punish genocide is widely accepted as a principle of customary law."

[118] Article 6(c) of the Charter of the International Military Tribunal for the Trial of the Major War Criminals stated that crimes against humanity were "within the jurisdiction of the Tribunal, whether or not in violation of the domestic law of the country where perpetrated." As the U.S. Sixth Circuit Court explained in the case of Demanjanjuk v. Petrovsky, 776 F.2d 571, 582 (6th Cir. 1985), referring to Nuremberg: "it is generally agreed that the establishment of these tribunals and their proceedings were based on universal jurisdiction."

[119] *Attorney General of Israel* v. *Eichmann,* in *International Law Review,* vol. 36, p.50 (Israel District Court, Jerusalem 1961), hereinafter *Eichmann.* The District Court of Jerusalem explained how "the State of Israel's 'right to punish' the accused derives... from two cumulative sources: a universal source (pertaining to the whole of mankind) which vests the right to prosecute and punish crimes of this order in every state within the family of nations; and a specific national source...." Israel's Supreme Court found, similarly, that there was "full justification for applying here the principal of universal jurisdiction since the international character of "crimes against humanity"... dealt with in this instant case is no longer in doubt..." (Israel Supreme Court, 1962)

[120] *British Manual of Military Law,* cited in M. Cherif Bassiouni, *Crimes Against Humanity in International Criminal Law* (Netherlands: Martinus Nijhoff Publishers, 1992), p.520.

[121] See, for example, Frits Kalshoven, *The Law of Warfare,* (1973), p.119, cited in Theodor Meron, "International Criminalization of Internal Atrocities," *American Journal of International Law,* vol.89, (July 1995), p.572, which states that "in customary international law, jurisdiction over war criminals is universal." Also the *Restatement,* ibid, lists "piracy, slave trade, attacks on or hijacking of aircraft, genocide, *war crimes,* and perhaps certain acts of terrorism... *(emphasis added)*" as subject to universal jurisdiction.

specifically provide for universal jurisdiction over grave breaches.[122] It is now established that such jurisdiction applies in respect of a range of crimes beyond grave breaches, to crimes committed in international and internal armed conflict.[123] Some commentators that have noted that the fundamental guarantees of Protocol II are "obviously a matter of 'international concern' and therefore also covered by universal jurisdiction."[124] As one commentator noted, "[o]nce internal atrocities are recognized as international crimes and thus as matters of major international concern, the right of third states to prosecute violators must be accepted."[125]

For certain of the war crimes included in the proposed list of crimes in section A, the existence of universal jurisdiction is less clear than for others. In this respect, the ICC statute should adopt a progressive approach, in line with trends towards broadening the scope of crimes under customary international law, particular in internal conflict and the reach of the principle of universal jurisdiction.[126] Delegations should recognize the historic opportunity that the creation an ICC represents, to endow the Court with the power necessary to combat impunity in respect of the very egregious crimes within its jurisdiction.

---

[122] The common articles of the Geneva Conventions, ibid, include the statement that "Each High Contracting Party shall be under the obligation to search for persons alleged to have committed, or to have ordered to be committed, such grave breaches [of the present Convention], and shall bring such persons, regardless of their nationality, before its own courts..."

[123] For example, Article 3 was held to be subject to universal jurisdiction in the Military and Paramilitary Activities in and Against Nicaragua case (*Nicaragua* v. *United States*), *International Court of Justice*, (1994), p.392.

[124] Meron, "International Criminalization of Internal Atrocities," p.559.

[125] Meron, ibid., p.576.

[126] Acknowledging developments in the area of law, Professor Meron writes: "until very recently, the accepted wisdom was that neither common Article 3 (which is not among the grave breaches provisions of the Geneva Conventions) nor Protocol II (which contains no provisions on grave breaches) provided a basis for universal jurisdiction, and that they constituted, at least on the international plane, an uncertain basis for individual criminal responsibility. Meron, "International Criminalization of Internal Atrocities," p.559.

RECOMMENDATION ON ARTICLES 6, 7 AND 9

Articles 6, 7 and 9

- *Recommendation:* **The statute should establish that the Court may exercise its jurisdiction with respect to a crime falling within its jurisdiction, if one of the mechanisms capable of triggering the Court's jurisdiction has been invoked in accordance with the provisions of the statute.[127] There should be no additional pre-requisite to the exercise of jurisdiction. The acceptance of the Court's jurisdiction should be inherent in the ratification of the statute. There should be no possibility of "selecting" from among the core crimes, nor of accepting or withholding acceptance on a case-by-case basis. Non-state parties should be able to accept the Court's jurisdiction over a particular case for the purpose of assuming the obligations under the statute; the consent of non-state parties should not, however, be a prerequisite to the Court's exercise of jurisdiction.**

Comment: The purpose of an international criminal court is to bring to justice perpetrators of egregious crimes. Through ratifying the statute, states should confer on the Court the jurisdiction to fulfil this mandate. As the crimes in question are of universal concern and should be subject to universal jurisdiction, the ICC should be able to prosecute these crimes, as any of the states ratifying the statute might, without any requirement of state consent.

Opt-in regime: the 'selection' of core crimes

Under Article 7, Option 1 of the statute, the Court will only have automatic jurisdiction over genocide.[128] It will be able to exercise jurisdiction over crimes against humanity and war crimes only where all of the following states have accepted the Court's jurisdiction over the specific crime(s) in question: the custodial state, the state on whose territory the crime was allegedly committed, a state that has requested surrender of the suspect, the state of nationality of the victim, and the state of nationality of the suspect. In addition to providing states with the option to be selective in deciding which crimes they wish to recognize the Court's jurisdiction

---

[127] For recommendations on specific trigger mechanisms, see Section D of this document.

[128] We note that the proposal at Article 9, Option 2, even envisions removing genocide from the Court's inherent jurisdiction.

over,[129] Article 9 provides for the further option of recognizing the Court's jurisdiction of "particular conduct," or "for a specified period of time."[130] This would result in what certain delegates refer to as the "a la carte" approach to the jurisdiction of the Court.

As noted above, universal jurisdiction applies to genocide, crimes against humanity and war crimes. Distinguishing between these core crimes, or allowing states to pick and choose, is as legally unjustifiable as it is offensive to the egregious nature of all of these offences.

Moreover, on a practical level, as crimes against humanity and war crimes almost always accompany genocide, a Court which has the competence to try the latter crime should have the competence to try the former crimes. Much of the investigation and evidence will overlap for these crimes in any given situation, so trying them together has the advantage of efficiency. An "a la carte" approach would lead to confusion as to the scope of the Court's jurisdiction and to the Court having jurisdictions over different crimes for different offenders. It would further run the risk that crimes would not be prosecuted in the most appropriate way–a given act may be prosecuted as one crime over which the Court's jurisdiction is accepted by all the relevant states when it would more appropriately be characterized as another within the Court's jurisdiction, but in respect of which acceptance has been withheld.[131]

---

[129] This would appear to allow states to not only select between genocide, crimes against humanity and war crimes for the purpose of recognizing the jurisdiction of the Court, but also to select particular acts within these categories for the same purpose. The obvious risk is that states will simply not accept jurisdiction over the crimes that they or other "friendly" states will be accused of committing, thus avoiding the Court's jurisdiction while receiving the political gain of being seen to be party to the ICC statute and generally accepting the jurisdiction of the Court.

[130] Article 9, Option 2, paragraphs (2) and (3) respectively.

[131] For example, if someone commits torture and a state does not recognize the Court's jurisdiction for torture but does for bodily injury, while a prosecution can quite properly proceed in respect of the latter, it would not be the most appropriate basis for a prosecution of the conduct in question. This invites the development of confusion and uncertainty in the Court's practice and jurisprudence, and could jeopardize the principle of legal certainty.

We therefore urge delegates to adopt an approach in line with Article 7 of the "further option for Articles 6, 7, 10 and *11[10 bis]*,"[132] and include no provision for accepting jurisdiction over particular crimes or for particular conduct.

State consent in individual cases

Particularly inconsistent with the notion of an effective and independent court is the proposal that specified state parties should be required to consent to the exercise of the Court's jurisdiction in particular cases.[133] Article 7, Option 2 provides for all of the following states to have to have "accepted the exercise of the jurisdiction of the Court with respect to the case in question": the state of custody, the state on whose territory the crimes were committed, any state that has requested surrender of the suspect, the state of nationality of the victim and nationality of the suspect or accused.[134]

Such a provision, which contains no limitations on the grounds on which that consent might be granted or withheld, invites interference with justice in politically "inconvenient" cases. Requiring the state on whose territory the crime is committed, for example, or of the nationality of the suspect, to "consent" to the jurisdiction of the Court renders illusory hopes for an effective court. Such a provision flouts the reality that the worst war criminals are often protected by, or indeed act on behalf of, states. Delegations are urged in the strongest terms to oppose the inclusion of any such provision.

The proposal that a state might at the same time accept the Court's jurisdiction over all crimes through ratification, but then be required to "consent" or not consent to the exercise of that jurisdiction on a case-by-case basis, is absurd. The ability to subsequently withhold consent renders meaningless the original supposed "acceptance" of the Court's jurisdiction.

----

[132] This further option is based on a proposal submitted by the delegation of the United Kingdom.

[133] Note that one proposal within paragraph 3 of the second option of Article 7, provides that if one of the states has not indicated whether it gives such acceptance, the Court may *not* exercise jurisdiction; this would establish a presumption against the Court's ability to function.

[134] Each of the states listed is in brackets, as is entire Option 2.

In this respect, as in the foregoing provision on the selection of crimes, Article 7 of the "further option for Articles 6, 7, 10 and 11[10 *bis*]"[135] is favorable since it contains no provision for state party consent.

Non- state parties and the exercise of jurisdiction

Consent should not be a prerequisite to the exercise of jurisdiction. The proposal put forward in the Article 9 "further option"[136] which would not require the consent of any states, party or non-party, to establish the Court's jurisdiction per se,[137] should be supported. There is support for this view in international law, which would allow state parties through the statute to confer on the Court the power to exercise jurisdiction over these crimes of universal jurisdiction. Moreover, the provisions of the statute in this respect are critical to ensuring that perpetrators of these very serious crimes be brought to justice.

On the question of non-state parties, it is critical to distinguish between establishing jurisdiction of the ICC, and establishing the duty of states to cooperate with the Court. Non-state parties are not bound by a statute which they have not ratified: they have no duties towards the Court. The ICC could not enter the territory of non-state party without its consent, for example, and could not demand transfer of an accused.

Since the ICC will depend on states' cooperation in order to fulfil its investigatory and prosecutorial mandate, this may in certain cases signify that, where a non-state party refuses to recognize the Court's jurisdiction and thereby agree to cooperate, an investigation will not, in practice, come to fruition. But this is a practical question of cooperation, not a legal basis for limiting the Court's jurisdiction. Moreover, it is not necessarily the case that prosecution will be impossible in the circumstances outlined. In the theoretical situation where both the state of custody and the state of territory are non-state parties and refuse to cooperate in a particular case, sufficient evidence may be available in third states which *are* cooperating with

---

[135] This further option is based on a proposal submitted by the delegation of the United Kingdom.

[136] This option was the proposal of the Federal Republic of Germany, presented at the sixth Preparatory Committee for the Establishment of an International Criminal Court.

[137] On this point alone do we depart from the provisions of the "further option" referred to above.

the Court. The suspect might leave the state in which he or she is absconding and go to another state, at which stage he or she could be brought within the reach of the Court. The importance of prosecuting these egregious crimes demands that this possibility be available to the Court.

Requiring the consent of either or both the state of custody and the state of territory, as required by the "further option for Articles 6, 7, 10 and 11[10 *bis*],"[138] is unjustifiable. Given that any state might exercise jurisdiction over these crimes, under universal jurisdiction, there is no convincing legal justification for distinguishing the territorial and custodial states, as states whose consent is required, from any other state.[139] In any event, no state's consent should be necessary to prosecute egregious crimes of universal jurisdiction: the international community already shares the interest and in many cases the obligation to do so. The legal integrity of the statute underpinning the establishment of the Court demands that this particular manifestation of the requirement of state consent be deleted.

Ability of Non-State Parties to Recognize the Jurisdiction of the Court

Non-state parties wishing to accept the jurisdiction of the court on an ad hoc basis, for example so as to have the right to refer cases to the court, should be able to do so. In doing so, they must thereby assume the duty of cooperation under Part 9 of the statute, as provided for in Article 7(3) of the "further option for Articles 6, 7, 10 and 11[10 *bis*]." Consistent with the position set out above, states consent would relate to their assumption of the obligations under the statute, but would not be a prerequisite to jurisdiction.

---

[138] The United Kingdom proposal.

[139] If the basis upon which their consent is required is that they themselves have jurisdiction, according to universal jurisdiction, all states should have to consent, thus ensuring the unequivocal paralysis of the ICC. If the justification is the practical point addressed in the preceding paragraph, this is not a basis for excluding jurisdiction, but is a cooperation question dealt with elsewhere in the statute.

JURISDICTION OVER MINORS

* *Recommendation:* **The International Criminal Court should have no jurisdiction over persons who were under the age of eighteen at the time they are alleged to have committed a crime which would otherwise come within the jurisdiction of the Court.**[140]

Comment: The punitive purpose of the Court is fundamentally at odds with the rehabilitative purpose of international standards on juvenile justice. Children accused of committing crimes are entitled under international law to adjudication by specialized juvenile justice systems, whose principle goal is rehabilitation and promotion of the well-being and best interests of the young person, rather than retribution.[141] The Court, however, is conceived of as an extraordinary court, to try persons charged with committing or ordering the most egregious offenses. It serves an essentially punitive function, the primary penalty being imprisonment, and is therefore a wholly inappropriate forum for the adjudication of children.

---

[140] This proposal was put forward by delegations during the December 1997 PrepCom, and is referenced in footnote 3 of A/AC.249/1998/CRP.13, on applicable penalties. Rather than treating the issue as one of establishing an age of responsibility, delegates proposed that the matter be approached as a jurisdictional issue, and proposed that the Court not have jurisdiction over persons under the age of eighteen. Human Rights Watch supports this approach.

[141] *See* Convention on the Rights of the Child, Article 40(1); U.N. Standard Minimum Rules for the Administration of Juvenile Justice ("Beijing Rules"), Articles 5.1, 14.2, 17.1, 26; International Covenant on Civil and Political Rights, Articles 10(3) and 14(4); American Convention on Human Rights, Article 5(5); European Convention for the Protection of Human Rights and Fundamental Freedoms, Article 5(1)(d); African Charter on the Rights and Welfare of the Child, Article 17(3). The Commentary to Article 17 of the Beijing Rules is particularly on point: "Whereas in adult cases, and possibly also in cases of severe offences by juveniles, just desert and retributive sanctions might be considered to have some merit, in juvenile cases such considerations should always be outweighed by the interest of safeguarding the well-being and the future of the young person."

Much discussion has already focused on the age of criminal responsibility,[142] and on the related issue of sentencing of minors,[143] reflecting widely divergent views on the issues. We support the position of UNICEF and delegations that recommend the age of responsibility be set at eighteen years for crimes within the jurisdiction of the Court. However, rather than becoming enmeshed in attempting to agree on an age of criminal responsibility, on drawing up specialized procedural mechanisms for adjudicating minors, and on appropriate rehabilitative correctional measures for minors, the Court's limited resources would be far better used in pursuit of justice for more serious adult offenders.

As the report of the U.N. Secretary General's expert on the Impact of Armed Conflict on Children noted, children are rarely autonomous actors in the commission of crimes such as those covered by the statute.[144] Where appropriate, under the principle of command responsibility, the Court could impose accountability on those who knowingly disregarded the commission of crimes by their subordinates who were children.[145]

In cases where adults deliberately used persons under the age of eighteen to commit crimes within the jurisdiction of the Court, such gross exploitation of children

---

[142] Current proposals regarding the establishment of an absolute or presumptive age of criminal responsibility, range from setting the age at thirteen to twenty-one years. *See* A/CONF.183/2/Add.1, 14 April 1998, Article 26[20], on age of responsibility.

[143] The statute envisions imprisonment as the primary penalty, leaving open the possibility of life sentencing and even the death penalty for minors. This is incompatible with established international juvenile justice standards. While proposals also exist for special sentencing measures for young persons, Human Rights Watch finds them to be inadequate; one of the proposals sets 20 years as the maximum imprisonment term for persons under the age of eighteen. *See* A/CONF.183/2/Add.1, 14 April 1998, Article 75[68], on applicable penalties

[144] "One of the most disturbing and difficult aspects of children's participation in armed conflict is that, *manipulated by adults*, they may become perpetrators of war crimes including rape, murder, and genocide." Report of Graca Machel, Expert of the Secretary-General of the United Nations, on the impact of armed conflict on children, A/51/306, para. 250 [emphasis added].

[145] *See* A/CONF.183/2/Add.1, 14 April 1998, Article 25[19], on command responsibility.

should be considered as an aggravating factor in sentencing.[146] This would also deter adults from using children as instruments for the perpetration of crimes in order to escape criminal liability and accountability generally.

---

[146] The Working Group on Penalties incorporated "the use of minors in the commission of the crime" in a non-exhaustive list of factors to be considered by the Court in determination of the sentence. See A/AC.249/1997/WG.6/CRP.3/Rev, on determination of the sentence. Article 26[20] of the draft statute, A/CONF.183/2/Add.1, on determination of the sentence, does not contain the non-exhaustive list of factors. We recommend that the use of minors in the commission of the crime should be considered as a factor in assessing "the gravity of the crime," as should the targeting of children as victims of crimes.

SECTION C: ROLE OF THE SECURITY COUNCIL

The role of the Security Council, as delineated in Article 10, and its relationship to the Court, raises several difficult questions. Given its primary role under the United Nations Charter for maintaining international peace and security, the Council should have an important role in referring cases to the Court. However, Article 10(3), which would give the Security Council control over the Court's ability to exercise its jurisdiction in cases arising out of a situation being dealt with by the Security Council under its Chapter VII powers, constitutes a serious threat to the independence of the Court. Subjecting the Court to the control of the Security Council -- and to its highly political decision-making process -- would have a profoundly negative impact on the Court's ability to function independently, as well as on its legitimacy, authority and credibility.

REFERRALS BY THE SECURITY COUNCIL

Article 10(1)

• *Recommendation 1:* **The Security Council should be empowered to refer matters to the ICC, pursuant to a "decision" by the Council, acting under Chapter VI or VII of the U.N. Charter.**

Comment: Article 10(1) grants the Court jurisdiction over crimes arising in the context of matters referred to the Court by the Security Council. The Security Council has a duty to maintain international peace and security, including upholding international law, for which referral power to the ICC is essential.

The establishment of a permanent international criminal court should eliminate the need for the Security Council to establish ad hoc tribunals in the future. Only if the ICC is capable of fulfilling the function that such tribunals might fulfill--if the Security Council can confer powers on the ICC and oblige states, in accordance with the U.N. Charter,[147] on the same basis as it would through the establishment of an ad hoc tribunal--will the need for future ad hoc tribunals be truly obviated.

When the Security Council refers a matter to the Court, member states should be bound to give effect to that decision, through cooperation with the Court, just as all member states of the U.N. are bound to cooperate with the International Criminal

---

[147] The Charter of the United Nations, June 26, 1945, 59 Stat. 1031, U.N. Treaty Series No.993.

Tribunals for the Former Yugoslavia and Rwanda and comply with its requests and judgments.[148] Article 10(1) should therefore refer to a "decision" of the Security Council: member states of the U.N. are obliged under the Charter to "accept and carry out" "decisions" of the Council, under Article 25 of the U.N. Charter,[149] and to give priority to those obligations over other inconsistent obligations, under Article 103.[150]

As such, when the Security Council is dealing with a matter, whether under Chapter VI or Chapter VII, and it is brought to its attention that a crime within the jurisdiction of the Court may have been committed, it should be able to refer that matter to the Court under either Chapter, provided that binding nature of that decision is clear.[151]

That said, the commission of such grave crimes as those within the jurisdiction of the Court, and the impunity that so often surrounds them, almost always constitute a "threat to peace, [or a] breach of peace," as envisioned in Chapter VII. As such, the decision to refer matters to the Court should, in general, be taken under that

---

[148] Article 29 of the statute of the ICTY, for example, obliges all member states to cooperate with that tribunal.

[149] Article 25 of the U.N. Charter reads: "The Members of the United Nations agree to accept and carry out the decisions of the Security Council in accordance with the present Charter."

[150] Article 103 of the U.N. Charter reads: " In the event of a conflict of the obligations of the Members of the United Nations under the present Charter and their obligations under any other international agreement, their obligations under the present Charter shall prevail."

[151] The binding nature of decisions is not determined by whether they are taken under Chapter VI or Chapter VII, but by whether they were intended to bind all member states. See, for example, Rosalyn Higgins, "The Advisory Opinion on Namibia: which Resolutions are Binding under Article 25 of the Chapter?," *International and Comparative Law Quarterly*, vol.21, p.280. The author states that the Charter offers no support for the view that Article 25 applies only to measures under Chapter VII, but rather applies to "all decisions of the Security Council adopted in accordance with the Charter." The ICJ's advisory opinion on the "Legal Consequences for States of the Continued Presence of South Africa in Namibia (South West Africa), Notwithstanding Security Council Resolution 276," 1971 ICJ Rep.4-345 (1970), indicates that a range of factors may point to the intention to bind member states of the U.N., and that the Chapter under which it is passed is not definitive of the binding nature of a resolution.

chapter of the Charter.[152] If, however, the commission of a crime within the Court's jurisdiction comes to the attention of the Council in circumstances which are not deemed to constitute a threat to international peace and security, it should not be precluded from referring the matter to the Court. What is essential is that the binding nature of a Security Council decision is clear.

SECURITY COUNCIL CONTROL OVER CASES BEFORE THE COURT

Article 10(7)

- *Recommendation:* **The Security Council should not be able to interfere with and prevent the exercise of the Court's jurisdiction.**

Comment: The International Court of Justice (ICJ) expressed the relationship between itself and the Security Council in the following terms:
"The Council has powers of a political nature...whereas the Court exercises purely judicial functions. The organs can therefore perform their separate but complimentary functions with respect to the same events."[153]

It went on to state that:
"The fact that a matter is before the Security Council should not prevent it being dealt with by the Court and that both proceedings can be pursued *pari passu*."[154]

These statements apply with equal if not greater force to an international criminal court with functions quite separate from the political functions of the Council, but very much complimentary in the protection of international peace and security. The argument that ICC jurisdiction may interfere with the promotion of peace

---

[152] Moreover, the intention to bind would be more readily assumed if the decision were made under Chapter VI. This is particularly so in the light of the "Case Concerning Questions of Interpretation and Application of the 1971 Montreal Convention Arising from Aerial Incident at Lockerbie (Libya v.USA) 1998," International Court of Justice, February 29, 1998. The International Court of Justice, while not stating that *only* decisions under Chapter VII are binding, clearly considered the fact that it was an exercise of Chapter VII power a relevant factor in determining whether or not a particular resolution was intended to bind.

[153] Ibid, pp.443-4.

[154] "Military and Paramilitary Activities in and Against Nicaragua (Nicaragua v. United States),"International Court of Justice, (1984), p.433.

agreements is spurious.[155] Rather, any suggestion that the Court's jurisdiction might be used as a negotiable element in any potential peace agreement brokered by the Council should be rejected, on the basis that it would inevitably seriously diminish the Court's stature, politicize its role and, hence, undermine its credibility.

Just as the International Court of Justice has jurisdiction to consider cases whether or not they arise from situations being dealt with by the Security Council under its Chapter VII powers,[156] the ICC should not be precluded for exercising jurisdiction because the Security Council is dealing with a matter.

Option one: the operation of security council veto

Option 1 of Article 10(7) would prevent the Court from exercising jurisdiction in cases arising out of situations being dealt with by the Security Council, unless the Council expressly permitted the Court to do so. This would allow any one permanent member of the Council to veto the exercise of the Court's jurisdiction, and must be adamantly opposed. This option would reduce the ICC from an independent judicial body to a subordinate body of the Security Council and render justice hostage to the political whims of the permanent members of the Security Council.

Advancing the rule of law internationally, which is one of the fundamental underlying goals of the establishment of the ICC, requires a judicial system that is truly independent. Independence is essential to ensure that justice is done, and that the ICC is a credible judicial institution, clearly beyond the political influence of even the most powerful states. This is clearly not compatible with five individual states enjoying veto power over which cases fall within the Court's docket.

---

[155] The peace process in the former Yugoslavia, which took place while efforts were made to bring to justice those responsible for atrocities in the region, demonstrates this.

[156] In the "Legal Consequences for States of the Continued Presence of South Africa in Namibia" case, the ICJ gave an advisory opinion on the legality of a General Assembly resolution determining that South Africa's presence in Namibia was illegal, while the matter was on the agenda of the Security Council and had been subject to several resolutions by that body. Likewise in "Certain Expenses of the United Nations," (1962, ICJ 151) the ICJ gave an advisory opinion, at the behest of the General Assembly, on whether member state were obliged, by virtue of a Security Council resolution, to pay the expenses of U.N. operations in the Congo and the Middle East.

Option two: a decision of the security council to suspend ICC jurisdiction

Option 2 of Article 10(7) provides that the Security Council acting under Chapter VII may take a decision that no ICC prosecution may be commenced (or proceeded with). While this option would not permit the operation of the veto by any one state to exclude a case from the Court, it still involves an inevitable loss of judicial independence by allowing a political body absolute power to interfere with the administration of justice. As noted above, the Council does not enjoy such a power vis à vis cases before the International Court of Justice.

Moreover, in the current draft of Option 2, there is no limit on the length of time the ICC could be prevented from exercising its jurisdiction. It presently contains a bracketed option at paragraph 1, which prevents the Court exercising jurisdiction for a period of twelve months; however, at paragraph 2 this period may be extended "at intervals of 12 months." The scope which this allows for unlimited extensions and indefinite suspension of jurisdiction over these very serious crimes gives serious cause for concern.

The option states that "[N]o prosecution may be commenced [*or proceeded with*]... [emphasis added]" where the Security Council has decided to that effect. With this wording retained, even once an ICC prosecution was underway, the Security Council could step in and call a halt to proceedings when it serves the political interests of the states involved in the Security Council decision to do so.

Bracketed paragraph 3 of the option would be an appropriate addition to Option 2, enabling the ICC to exercise jurisdiction where, after a reasonable period, the Security Council is not in fact taking any action in respect of the situation in question.

While the susceptibility to political abuse is greatly reduced where a decision of the Council as a whole is required, as in Option 2, rather than control lying with the decision of particular individual states, as in Option 1, both options conspire against the independence of the Court.

SECTION D: HOW AN INVESTIGATION IS TRIGGERED

Once an ICC is established, it is essential that when one of the egregious crimes within its subject matter jurisdiction is committed and national authorities do not investigate, the Court is able to fulfil its mandate, carry out an investigation and, if appropriate, prosecute. States and the Security Council have important roles in bringing the commission of crimes to the attention of the prosecutor for this purpose. Of crucial importance to the effectiveness and independence of the Court, however, is the *ex officio* power of the ICC prosecutor. In this section we make recommendations as to necessary trigger mechanisms and, aware of concerns that delegations have expressed in relation to *ex officio* powers, we address those concerns directly. Finally, we comment on the appropriate scope for judicial review of the decision to investigate *ex officio*.

COMPLAINT BY STATES

State parties

Article 11 [45]: Complaint by all state parties

* **Recommendation: Any state party should be permitted to lodge a complaint with the prosecutor with regard to any crime within the subject matter jurisdiction of the Court.**

Comment: The current text of Article 11 [45] provides an unnecessarily complex range of options concerning which state parties should be able to refer cases to the prosecutor. The first option provides that a complaint may be lodged only by a state party that has accepted the jurisdiction of the Court in respect of the crime which is the subject of the complaint (or, in the case of genocide, is a party to the Genocide Convention). The second is even more restrictive in allowing only the state on whose territory the crime is committed, the state which has custody of suspects, the state of nationality of a suspect or of the victim to make such a compliant.

All state parties should be able to refer cases to the Court.[157] As the acceptance of the Court's jurisdiction over the core crimes should be automatic on ratification of the statute, the references in both options to state parties "which accept the jurisdiction of the Court" is redundant and should be deleted.

---

[157] See Recommendation 1 for Article 6, 7, and 9.

Non-state parties

Article 11[45]: Complaint by non-state parties

• **Recommendation 2: The statute should allow complaints to be made by non-state parties to the ICC, on the condition that a complaining non-state party recognize the competence of the Court and assume the obligations under the statute in respect of the investigation or prosecution of the matters which are the subject of the complaint.**

Comment: The current text of Article 11[45] allows only for complaint by "state parties."[158] The ICC should have the broadest possible access to information concerning the commission of crimes of concern to the international community as a whole. As such, we support the possibility of non-state party complaints. However, if non-state parties are entitled to make complaints on the same basis as state parties, it is essential that they should also assume the obligations incumbent upon state parties, for the purposes of the particular matter referred to the Court.

SECURITY COUNCIL

Article 10: Complaint by the Security Council

• **Recommendation: The Security Council should be empowered to refer a matter to the ICC.**

Comment: At part C of this Commentary, on the role of the Security Council, we indicated support for the power of the Council to refer matters to the Court, and readers are referred to that section.

EX OFFICIO POWERS OF THE PROSECUTOR

Article 12 [46]: Ex officio powers of the prosecutor

• **Recommendation: The prosecutor should be empowered to initiate investigations *ex officio* on the basis of information obtained from any source.**

---

[158] Note that Article 6 on the exercise of jurisdiction contemplates the lodging of complaints by non-state parties.

Comment: In order to establish an independent and effective Court it is absolutely essential that the prosecutor be empowered to initiate investigations *ex officio* on the basis of reliable information. The contribution of information from victims is of particular importance and would be especially valuable in bringing perpetrators to justice. If only states and the Security Council can trigger prosecutorial investigations, the proper functioning of the Court will be dependant on the political motivations of these entities. This exposes the Court to the risk that only individuals or nationals of states that have fallen out of favor will be prosecuted, rather than those responsible for the most egregious crimes.

History bears witness to the reality that, in practice, states or the Council will often be reluctant or unable to lodge complaints or refer situations to the Court. The inter-state complaint mechanism in human rights instruments is vastly underutilized:[159] no state complaints having been brought to the Inter-American Court of Human Rights, nor to the Human Rights Committee under the International Covenant on Civil and Political Rights,[160] and only one inter-state case has been heard by the European Court of Human Rights.[161] Similarly, only one case alleging violation of the Genocide Convention has ever been brought before the International Court of Justice.

The factors which one commentator has suggested may account for this are the impact on inter-state economic and political relations and the fear of counterclaims.[162] Even where states want to bring claims, for example a state after a transition may wish to complain to the ICC regarding atrocities during the previous regime, it will often be under enormous internal pressure not to do so.

---

[159] See Scott Leckie, "The Inter-State Complaint Procedure in International Human Rights Law: Hopeful Prospects or Wishful Thinking," *Human Rights Quarterly*, vol.10, (1988), p.302, for a helpful chart detailing use of state-to-state complaint procedures in various human rights bodies.

[160] Article 41 of theInternational Covenant on Civil and Political Rights, adopted by the General Assembly on December 16, 1966 and entered into force on March 23, 1976. G.A. Res. 2200, U.N. GAOR, 21st Session, Supp. No. 16, at 52, 59, U.N. Doc. A/6316 (1966), 999 U.N. Treaty Series 171, 301 (1967).

[161] *Ireland* v. *the United Kingdom* (ECHR 5310/71).

[162] Leckie, "The Inter-State Complaint Procedure...," p.254.

This, coupled with the fact that any one permanent member of the Security Council would be able to prevent Security Council referral, runs the risks that inaction or lack of political will on the part of states and Security Council could, in practice, continue to protect perpetrators of very serious crimes from accountability.

Moreover, the statute as presently drafted would appear to restrict the Court's jurisdiction to the crimes or individuals specified in the state complaint or Security Council referral. For example, the complaint may restrict the investigation to particular crimes, committed by particular individuals, under one regime or during a specified time period, for example, in a way that would skew the prosecutor's ability to conduct a thorough investigation. Strong *ex officio* powers are essential to ensure that the prosecutor enjoys the independence and flexibility necessary for the effective carrying out of his or her functions.

The ability of the prosecutor to independently respond to allegations of egregious crimes is essential for the independent administration of justice. An international criminal court that could not investigate a case of genocide, for example, in the face of overwhelming information from victims and survivors, because of the absence of state or Security Council complaint, would be of questionable legitimacy.

Addressing concerns regarding a proprio motu prosecutor

Human Rights Watch is concerned by the opposition on the part of certain states to the inclusion of a prosecutorial power to investigate *proprio motu* which is an indispensable attribute of any independent prosecutor. The prosecutor will be a very experienced professional person of the highest standing and moral character.[163] In the unlikely event that the prosecutor proves to abuse the power afforded to him or her, or to be incompetent, he or she will be subject to removal from office[164] or lesser disciplinary measures,[165] in accordance with Part 4 of the statute.

If incompatible with the principle of complementarity, which ensures the highest deference to national authorities, the investigation will not proceed, and if it does, it can be challenged. Further, Article 13 [46], entitled "Information submitted to

---

[163] See Article 43 [36] of the current text.

[164] Article 47 [39].

[165] Article 48 [39 *bis*].

the Prosecutor,"[166] on which specific comments are made below[67] effectively provides for the Pre-Trial Chamber to screen the decision by the prosecutor to initiate an investigation. If this article prevails, it renders even less credible the assertion that an *ex officio* prosecutor poses a real threat of politically motivated or otherwise inappropriate investigations.

PRE-TRIAL CHAMBER REVIEW OF THE DECISION TO INVESTIGATE EX OFFICIO

Article 13 [2nd 46] : Information submitted to the prosecutor

- **Recommendation:** If the decision of the prosecutor to initiate an investigation is subject to judicial review, the standard by which the decision is judged must not go above the existence of a "reasonable basis" to proceed with an investigation.

Comment: This provision would allay any legitimate concerns that may exist concerning the dangers associated with *ex officio* powers. Judicial review of the decision to commence an investigation provides strong guarantees of fairness and propriety on the part of the prosecutor's office, and would therefore serve the important function of shielding the prosecutor from the detrimental effects of unfounded allegations as to impropriety, thus protecting the integrity and reputation of the Court.

It is critical, however, that the standard established is appropriate to the preliminary stage at which review will be taking place. It would be entirely inappropriate, for example, for the prosector to be expected to prove a prima facie case or probable cause at this stage, before initiating any investigation into the facts. We believe that new Article 13[2nd 46] sets an appropriate standard, by providing that the prosecutor must satisfy the Pre-Trial Chamber that a "reasonable basis" exists to proceed with an investigation.

Article 13[2nd 46] explicitly gives an important role to victims and organizations representing them, not only to present information to the prosecutor but also to make representations to the Pre-Trial Chamber. This is of fundamental importance

---

[166] The proposal which was submitted to the March-April Preparatory Committee by the delegations of Argentina and Germany appears as Article 13[2nd 46] in the latest text.

[167] See the following recommendation.

to the fulfilment of the Court's mandate to provide redress to victims of the egregious offences within its jurisdiction.

Finally, it is appropriate that Article 13[2nd 46](2) and (3) clarify that a finding by the Pre-Trial Chamber, or a decision by the prosecutor, that the investigation should not proceed precludes neither the reconsideration of the matter by the prosecutor, nor its resubmission to the chamber in the light of new facts or evidence.

SECTION E: COMPLEMENTARITY

Introduction

The codification and application of the statute's complementarity principle, governing the relationship between national jurisdictions and the Court, is key to the functioning of the International Criminal Court. On the one hand, the Court is not intended to be a supranational institution with the power to substitute itself for national legal systems. Rather, one by-product of an effective and independent Court should be to encourage national authorities themselves to investigate the crimes within the jurisdiction of the Court, and the consequent strengthening of national judicial systems. At the same time, the statute must ensure that, when national systems do not do so, the ICC is able to investigate and prosecute. It must be borne in mind that the impetus for the establishment of the ICC is the stark failure of national court systems to hold the perpetrators of genocide, crimes against humanity, and war crimes accountable under law.

Considerable time and effort was dedicated at the August 1997 Preparatory Committee session to the careful negotiation of the standard on which the Court will decide on the admissibility of cases before it. Delegates achieved agreement on the largely unbracketed text for Article 15[11] which provides extremely strong assurances that national authorities will remain the first line of investigation and prosecution. At the December Preparatory session, developments were made on the procedural aspects of admissibility challenges, in Article 17[12] of the statute. At the March-April 1998 Preparatory Committee session, one delegation proposed an Article *16[11 bis]* which provides for the application of the complementarity principle at an earlier phase of the process, prior to the commencement of an investigation.[168]

This section of the commentary offers recommendations and comments on Articles 15[11], 17[12], and *16[11 bis]*.

THE COMPLEMENTARITY TEST

Article 15[11]

- *Recommendation:* **A case should be inadmissible before the ICC where it is being or has been investigated or prosecuted by a state. The exception**

---

[168] This proposal was presented by the delegation of the United States.

to this rule should be where the national proceedings are "ineffective" or "unavailable," rather than where the state is "unwilling" or "unable."

Comment: Article 15[11], which deals with the substantive content of admissibility challenges, is the cornerstone of the complementarity principle. It is appropriate that complementarity be enshrined in clear terms in the statute to ensure that the ICC does not supplant the role of national authorities in the administration of criminal justice. However, the current text of Article 15[11] goes beyond ensuring that the ICC be able to investigate or prosecute only where national authorities do not in fact do so. It sets an unduly high threshold which may prevent ICC jurisdiction even in cases where there is no effective investigation and prosecution at the national level.

In the text of Article 15[11], a case is inadmissible where it is being or has been investigated or prosecuted by a state with jurisdiction, *unless* there is "inability" or "unwillingness" on the part of that state to genuinely carry out such an investigation or prosecution. What constitutes "unwillingness" or "inability" in this context is set out in an exhaustive list of criteria.

In each case the burden rests with the Court to demonstrate that no such proceedings exist and, if there is any question as to the existence of a national investigation or prosecution, to determine the inability or unwillingness of the state. In order to determine "inability" the Court must consider whether, due to "a total or partial collapse" or "unavailability" of its national judicial system, the state has been unable to carry out its proceedings. Further, in order to establish "unwillingness," the Court must demonstrate the underlying intent of the national authorities.[169] One concern, on a practical level, is the difficulty for the Court to gain access to information regarding a criterion as subjective as the intent of state authorities. In addition, this standard means that the Court would have to investigate and make subjective assessments as to the willingness of state authorities to bring to justice the perpetrators of serious violations. Ironically, the desire to avoid creating an ICC which sits in judgment of national authorities was

---

[169]Note that to determine "unwillingness" the Court will consider whether the proceedings had the purpose of shielding the person from criminal responsibility, or there has been undue delay inconsistent with the intent to bring the person to justice, or the proceedings were not conducted independently or impartially and were conducted in a manner inconsistent with the intent to bring the person to justice.

the justification given by certain states for seeking a strong provision on complementarity.

The present draft significantly raises the threshold for the exercise of jurisdiction by the ICC from the standard contained in the original ILC Draft Statute,[170] as reflected in the wording in the current draft preamble which provides that the ICC will be "complementary to national criminal justice systems in cases where such trial procedures may not be available or may be ineffective."[171] Unavailability and ineffectiveness are established standards used by human rights bodies to monitor whether domestic remedies have been exhausted as required for the exercise of jurisdiction of these bodies.[172] The criterion of "ineffectiveness" and "unavailability" provide not only an established but also an objective standard by which to assess the investigation or prosecution, rather than the more subjective criterion of "unwillingness" or "inability."

The text of Article 15[11] was achieved as a result of arduous negotiations during the August 1997 Preparatory Committee session. The extremely high standard for establishing admissibility provides ample assurance to states that their interests will not be infringed upon by the ICC and that the ICC will operate only in exceptional circumstances. In the light of these factors, it may be unlikely that states will want to reopen the language of Article 15[11]. Should they do so, however, effectiveness and availability should provide the relevant criterion by which the admissibility of cases before the ICC are judged.

---

[170] Article 6.

[171] See Preamble to the statute.

[172] The principle of exhaustion of "available" local remedies is set out in the International Covenant on Civil and Political Rights (ICCPR) which states, Article 41(1)(c), that "all available domestic remedies have been invoked and exhausted in the matter, in conformity with the generally recognized principles of international law." This is reflected in Article 26 of the European Convention for the Protection of Human Rights and Fundamental Freedoms and Article 46(1)(a) of the American Convention on Human Rights. Further, international bodies have determined that the general rule as to exhaustion of domestic remedies does not apply in circumstances in which domestic remedies are considered ineffective although available. See for example, the judgment of the Inter-American Court of Human Rights in *Godinez Cruz* Case, *Preliminary Objections, Judgment of June 26, 1987*, Inter-American Court of Human Rights, (Ser. D) No.3, (1994), para.95-7.

PROVISION FOR AMNESTY LAWS

Article 15[11]

One disturbing issue contained in Article 15[11], which remains unresolved, is the question of whether the Court should take into account national amnesty laws or pardons in determining admissibility of a case. One delegation raised the issue at the August 1997 Preparatory Committee session,[173] and circulated a paper on the issue. The new draft of Article 15[11] does not deal with the issue in the text of the article, but the provision does contain a footnote recognizing that certain issues, including "possibly also amnesties and pardons," should be revisited at an unspecified future stage.

- *Recommendation*: **Domestic legislation granting impunity for these heinous crimes should not be a basis for determining that a case before the ICC is inadmissible.**

Comment: There can be no recognition of legislation granting impunity for the crimes within the jurisdiction of the Court. There can be no "legitimate" amnesty for these crimes; rather, the application of an amnesty law to these offenses would be a clear contravention of established principles of international law.

There is a duty incumbent upon states to investigate and prosecute serious violations of international human rights and humanitarian law. In Article 1 of the Genocide Convention, this duty is explicit. Article 18 of the Declaration on the Protection of All Persons from Enforced Disappearance states that persons responsible for acts of enforced disappearance "shall not benefit from any special amnesty law or similar measure that might have the effect of exempting them from any criminal proceedings or sanction."[174] On several occasions, the U.N. Human

---

[173] The delegation of the United States of America.

[174] General Assembly Resolution 47/133 of December 18, 1992.

Rights Committee[175] and the Inter-American Commission on Human Rights[176] have made clear that the application of amnesty laws to serious human rights abuses is inconsistent with these international obligations. A special rapporteur of the U.N. Sub-Commission on the Prevention of Discrimination and Protection of Minorities also opposed the application of amnesties to serious violations of human rights.[177]

In light of the above, the inclusion in the statute of any deference to the application of amnesty laws to the crimes within the jurisdiction of the Court would be unacceptable. It would undermine the credibility and legitimacy of the Court--a body charged with upholding international law--if its statute were to allow a state to limit the Court's jurisdiction by taking measures which were themselves violations of international law.

National legislation granting impunity, far from rendering inadmissible the case before the International Criminal Court, may instead provide clear evidence of the *inability* or *unwillingness* of the national system to prosecute the crime.

A broad range of amnesty mechanisms have been adopted by states attempting to account for past violations, including those procedures more carefully crafted than blanket amnesties. However, given the exceptional nature of the Court's subject matter jurisdiction, these national efforts at exoneration should not affect the case's admissibility before the ICC.

---

[175] See, in particular, the U.N. Human Rights Committee Commentary on the Report of Argentina, April 5, 1995, where the Human Rights Committee determined that the Argentine amnesty law was incompatible with the requirements of the Covenant. It did so, on the basis that, inter alia, the law promoted an atmosphere of impunity for the authors of violations of human rights and consequently undermined the protection of those rights. *Comentarios al informe Argentino*, 5 April 1995, UN doc. CCPR/C/79/Add 46.

[176] The commission has reported on the illegality of amnesty laws in several cases. See in particular Reports 28/92 and 29/92 regarding the application of amnesty laws in Uruguay and Argentina respectively.

[177] Report of June 21, 1985, UN doc. E/CN.4/Sub.2/1985/16/Rev.1.

CHALLENGES TO ADMISSIBILITY UNDER ARTICLE 17[12]

Article 17[12]

Introduction

Article 17[12] deals with the procedure for challenging admissibility on the basis that the state is investigating or prosecuting pursuant to Article 15[11]. In this context, the procedural questions surrounding complementarity include who can challenge admissibility and when; what the interim consequences of a challenge should be; and who makes the ultimate decision on admissibility.[178] The task for delegates is to establish a statutory framework capable of ensuring that legitimate challenges to the exercise of jurisdiction can be made, without holding the functioning of the Court hostage to dilatory tactics and obstructionism.

Who can challenge

- *Recommendation 1*: **The right of a suspect to challenge admissibility should be removed. Only accused persons or interested states should be able to challenge.**

Comment: Article 17[12] contains an option which would allow an accused person or a suspect to challenge admissibility on grounds of complementarity. This option would open the door unnecessarily widely, and could lead to delays in the investigative phase. An individual who has been arrested clearly should, however, enjoy the right to challenge.

- *Recommendation 2*: **Only states whose interests are directly affected by the exercise of jurisdiction by the Court should be able to challenge admissibility. An interested state should be defined as a state which is carrying out the investigation or prosecution, by virtue of which admissibility is challenged.**

Comment: States directly interested or affected by the Court exercising its jurisdiction in the case should be able to challenge that exercise of jurisdiction on

---

[178] Within this framework, precise details of how challenges are to be made can be set out in the Rules of Procedure.

the basis of complementarity.[179] In this respect Article 17[12] should reflect Article *16[11 bis]*. The legitimate interest which complementarity seeks to address is the interest of the state in investigating or prosecuting the case; states that are doing so should therefore be able to challenge under Article 17[12]. On the other hand, states that are neither seeking nor intending to institute proceedings should not be able to delay ICC proceedings by challenging admissibility. Accordingly, the reference in Article 17[12](2)(b) granting the right to challenge to a state "which has received a request for cooperation" would allow states without a direct interest to challenge and should be deleted. It is states involved in any investigation or prosecution under Article 11 that would have access to the information concerning the domestic proceedings which would be necessary for the purposes of such a challenge, and challenge should be limited to such states.

Burden of proof

*   *Recommendation:*The burden of proof as to admissibility should lie with the state making the challenge. It must be for the state investigating or prosecuting, or which has done so, to furnish the Court with sufficient information as to the steps taken in such an investigation or prosecution to satisfy the Court that the exceptions as to the unwillingness or inability of the state do not apply.

Comment: It is inappropriate, in a challenge based on the *sufficiency* of national proceedings, for the burden of proof to be on the ICC prosecutor to demonstrate their *in*sufficiency. As most, if not all, of the relevant information about national proceedings would be in the hands of national authorities, not the ICC prosecutor, the burden of proof should be placed on the party best able to produce the relevant information - the state. On a practical level, for the ICC to ascertain what investigative or prosecutorial measures have been taken, and whether the state was willing and able to satisfy the Article 15[11] test, would impose a prohibitively onerous burden on the Court. Moreover, to give the ICC such a role would involve

---

[179] The "directly affected" formulation reflects Rule 108 of the Rules and Procedure of the International Criminal Tribunal for the Former Yugoslavia allowing states to appeal an interlocutory decision of the Tribunal where the state is "directly affected" by the decision. The Appeals Chamber, in its judgment of July 29, 1997, in the case of The Prosecutor v. Tihomir Blaskic, described Rule 108, which was adopted on July 24, 1997, in the following terms: "[t]he rule was adopted to fill a perceived lacuna in the Statute and Rules, namely that a state whose interests were intimately affected by a decision of the Trial Chamber could not request the Decision be submitted to appellate review."

the ICC in a considerable amount of investigation into national legal systems, which is not the intended remit of the Court.

Timing of challenges and right of appeal

• **Recommendation: Retain the provision allowing for states, unlike the accused, to challenge admissibility only prior to or at the commencement of trial, and only once. Similarly, retain the right of either party to appeal decisions on admissibility to the Appeals Chamber.**

Comment: Article 17[12](3) limits the opportunity for state challenges to admissibility to prior to or at the commencement of trial, and provides that challenges by states should, in general, be allowed only once. The provision correctly gives the Court discretion to allow a challenge to be brought more than once, or after the trial has begun, in exceptional circumstances. Such discretion is an important guarantee of flexibility for the Court on an essential issue relating to the implementation of the complementarity principle. Article 17[12] provides for the right of appeal by either party to the Appeals Chamber. These provisions should be retained, and the provisions of Article *16[11 bis]* be brought into line in respect of each of these points.[180]

Review in the light of new facts

• **Recommendation: The ability of the prosecutor to submit a subsequent request for a review of the decision on admissibility, in the light of new facts, should be retained.**

Comment: Delegates are urged to support the provision in bracketed paragraph 5, allowing the prosecutor to submit a request for review of the decision on the grounds that the conditions which rendered the case inadmissible no longer exist or that new facts have arisen.

Provisional measures

• **Recommendation: The statute should provide for the power of the prosecutor to take provisional measures, such as the preservation of evidence, pending resolution of the admissibility challenge.**

---

[180] See the section on Article 17[11 bis] below.

Comment: One bracketed provision of the current draft statute states that the prosecutor "shall not initiate an investigation where submission of the case is challenged under Article 15[11]...until the final ruling of the Court."[181] This could have serious implications if not coupled with the prosecutor's right to take such provisional measures as may be necessary to ensure that evidence is not lost or destroyed, pending resolution of a challenge to the admissibility of a case. Preservation may be essential if a subsequent prosecution is to be possible, in the event that the Court finds the case admissible. A challenge to admissibility must not be capable of paralyzing the Court and rendering impossible subsequent prosecutions where the challenge turns out to be unfounded. The inclusion of an express provision to this effect is necessary to clarify this important power.[182]

TRANSFER OF SUSPECTS FROM THE ICC UPON A FINDING OF INADMISSIBILITY BASED ON COMPLEMENTARITY

* **Recommendation: The statute should contain appropriate safeguards to ensure that, where the ICC decides to transfer a suspect to a state, following a determination of inadmissibility, it does so subject to the continued satisfaction of the complementarity test. The Court must be able to regain custody in the event of a subsequent determination that the conditions for inadmissibility no longer exist. The statute should make specific provisions in this regard for non-state parties, specifying that the transfer of a suspect to a non-state party should be contingent upon the state's recognition of the competence of the Court over the particular case, and its assumption of the obligation to transfer the suspect back to the Court upon a determination of admissibility.**

Comment: If the Court determines that a case is inadmissible, on the basis of complementarity, it may transfer a suspect in its custody to either a state party or a non-state party. However, safeguards must be taken to ensure that the Court could regain custody over the suspect if new circumstances rendered the case admissible before the Court and permitted the Court to assert jurisdiction over the suspect.

---

[181] See the bracketed option at Article 54(3)[47(1)*ter*].

[182] Such provision would correspond with the power which the Pre-Trial Chamber already enjoys, in the context of an investigation, to "take measures... to assure the efficiency and integrity of the proceedings...." It should be clear that this also applies where a decision on admissibility is pending.

The obligation of states parties to transfer persons to the Court, upon a request from the Court, are clearly set out in Part 9 of the statute. For non-state parties, however, there are no obligations vis à vis the Court. It is essential that if the Court relinquishes custody over a suspect upon the expectation, the requesting state will proceed with an investigation and prosecution; and if the state fails to do so, the Court must be able to regain custody over the suspect. Transfer should therefore be conditional upon acceptance by the non-state party of the obligation to return the suspect if the Court makes a subsequent determination that a case has been rendered admissible by the state's failure, inability, or unwillingness to investigate or prosecute.

During the earliest stages of the investigation, the Court may not yet have made a determination under Article 17[12] but, if proposed Article *16[11 bis]* is retained, may have deferred to the state investigation. Transfer would at that stage be premature. The ICC should, however, make the suspect available for questioning.

PRE-INVESTIGATION DETERMINATION OF COMPLEMENTARITY AND ADMISSIBILITY

Article 16[11 bis]

Introduction

Proposed Article *16[11 bis]*[183] is intended to apply at a preliminary stage, once the ICC prosecutor has determined that sufficient basis exists to launch an investigation. The procedures in Article *16[11 bis]* would enable a state to delay an ICC investigation unless the prosecutor determines -- and the Pre-Trial Chamber agrees -- that there has been a total or partial collapse of the state's legal system or that the state is unwilling or genuinely unable to carry out an investigation and prosecution. The decision to defer to a state investigation would not be able to be re-examined until six months or one year after the date of deferral.

Existing provisions safeguarding complementarity

Provisions ensuring the rigorous protection of the principle of complementarity are already incorporated into the statute. As stated above, a very high threshold for

---

[183] Article *16[11 bis]* was proposed on March 25, 1998, by the U.S. delegation. Unlike Article 15[11], this article was not discussed during the March/April Preparatory Committee session and does not represent the fruit of extensive negotiation and compromise.

admissibility is codified in Article 11. Prior to initiating an investigation the prosecutor must "determine whether... the case is or would be admissible under Article 15[11]...."[184] If the prosecutor so determines and the investigation does proceed, states that are genuinely investigating or prosecuting may challenge admissibility prior to or at the commencement of a trial, under Article 17[12]. Article 17[12] further obliges the Court to satisfy itself as to the admissibility of a case at all stages of the proceedings, on its own motion.

The legitimate scope of article 16 [11 bis]

In the light of these existing statutory protections of the complementarity principle, there is limited scope for further provisions to protect this principle. Human Rights Watch sees the legitimate scope of Article 11 *bis* as covering only the very preliminary stage at which it may be premature for the prosector or chamber of the Court to make any determination as to admissibility. At the moment when a matter is first referred to the Court, for example--such as shortly after the alleged commission of crimes within the Court's jurisdiction--even a state that is willing and able to investigate may not have taken sufficient investigative steps to satisfy the Court that it meets the complementarity test. There may therefore be some scope for the statute to provide for a conditional deferral, until such time as the Court is able to make a determination as to complementarity under Article 17[12]. The current text of Article *16[11 bis]* is too broadly formulated, inconsistent with other provisions of the statute and, most importantly, renders the Court susceptible to the obstruction of justice.

Certain of the following recommendations on Article *16[11 bis]* reflect those made in the context of Article 17[12], concerning the right to appeal and the appropriate burden of proof, while others reiterate the need for consistency between the two articles. The majority relate to specific concerns which would have to be addressed if delegates agree to some legitimate scope for Article *16[11 bis]*.

Public announcement

- *Recommendation*: **Limit pre-investigative notification to state parties, deleting the obligation of the prosecutor to make a public announcement prior to initiating an investigation.**

---

[184] See the current unbracketed text of Article 54[47].

Comment: Paragraph 1 of proposed Article *16[11 bis]* obliges the prosecutor to make a "public announcement" of his or her plans to initiate an investigation as well as notifying all states parties to the ICC statute.[185] As such, it goes beyond earlier proposals that state parties should be notified. A public announcement would involve notification not simply to states but also to suspects, which would entail certain obvious dangers. While we recognize that the announcement will provide information as to a "matter" and not specify which individuals are the subject of an investigation, it will often be clear from the facts given, and signal an opportunity for flight of suspects, tampering with evidence, or intimidation of witnesses.

Scope of article 16 [11 bis]

• **Recommendation: Article *16[11 bis]* should be brought into line with Article 17[12]. It should be clarified that Article *16[11 bis]* does not supersede Article 17[12], but rather operates only at a stage where a determination as to admissibility under that article is not appropriate.**

Comment: In situations where a state challenges admissibility claiming to be genuinely investigating or prosecuting a case, and that the case is inadmissible under Article 15[11], the procedure in Article 17[12] applies and the case will be deemed admissible or inadmissible. If Article *16[11 bis]* is retained, it should be clarified that it is intended to apply in those circumstances not covered by the scope of Article 17[12]. The scope of Article *16[11 bis]*, as identified in the introduction, should cover only the very preliminary stage at which a determination of admissibility is impossible or would be premature and therefore inappropriate.

Time restrictions on deferral

• **Recommendation: If the prosecutor defers investigation under Article *16[11 bis]*, he or she should be entitled to reopen the question of admissibility "at any time" if new facts indicate that the state is not satisfying the complementarity requirements set out in Article 15[11].**

Comment: Under the current text of the proposal, if the Court decides to defer to an investigation by the state and the prosecutor is unsuccessful in challenging this decision, the prosecutor may not seek to review this decision until a period of six months or a year has lapsed. By freezing the prosecutor's ability to act for six months or one year after the date of deferral, Article *16[11 bis]* provides ample

---

[185] See Article 54(2)(a)[47(1)bis(a)].

opportunity to destroy evidence and otherwise obstruct justice. This arbitrary time restriction should be deleted in favor of a provision that—consistent with Article 17[12]—allows a prosecutor who has deferred investigation to reopen the question of admissibility "at any time" if new facts indicate that the state is not satisfying the complementarity requirements set out in Article 15[11]. It would be anomalous to allow the ICC to reconsider the admissibility of a case at any time, where a deferral under Article 17[12] has been made, and impose a higher standard where the Court has deferred under Article *16[11 bis]*, in the absence of any prior determination that complementarity had in fact been met.

This flexibility is particularly important since Article *16[11 bis]* provides for deferral of a "situation" in general terms, not simply a case, a state may indeed be investigating a situation in general, but turn out not to investigate crucial aspects of it, or to pursue certain cases resulting from it.[186] The statute must not bar the ICC from the proper exercise of its jurisdiction where "situations," broadly formulated, are being investigated selectively or arbitrarily on the national level. At any time after a deferral to a state investigation, the Court should be able to make a determination as to complementarity and exercise its jurisdiction.

Preservation of evidence

• **Recommendation: In situations where an investigation is deferred according to Article *16[11 bis]*, the prosecutor must be allowed to take the steps necessary to preserve evidence, and for this purpose have access to both physical evidence and witnesses.**

Comment: If an ICC investigation is to be deferred under a modified Article *16[11 bis]*, deferral should be subject to the ICC prosecutor's right to preserve or safeguard evidence. For this purpose, deferral should be permitted only on the condition that the prosecutor be able to take steps as he or she deems necessary to prevent vital evidence from being compromised or lost. In some cases, when there is little reason to fear obstruction of justice, the ICC prosecutor could simply monitor national proceedings. In situations of greater risk, the ICC prosecutor would need direct access to physical evidence and the ability to conduct preliminary

---

[186] An example would be a case of genocide where the state decided to investigate only those immediately responsible, omitting investigation of those responsible for engineering the policy behind the acts, or the investigation of war crimes committed in a particular time or place but pursuing only crimes committed by one side and ignoring the other.

interviews of witnesses in order to preserve any evidence which would prove necessary for a case before the ICC should national proceedings fail.

Appeal

- **Recommendation 1: Allow the prosecutor to appeal any decision by the Pre-Trial Chamber to defer to the state.**

Comment: Contrary to Article 17[12](4), which provides that decisions on admissibility may be appealed by either party, paragraph 3 of proposed Article *16[11 bis]* apparently does not allow the prosecutor the opportunity to appeal a decision of the Pre-Trial Chamber to "defer" to the state for such a period. Article *16[11 bis]* should be brought into line with Article 17[12] in this respect.

- **Recommendation 2: The text should provide for expedited appeals**

Comment: The possibility of lengthy litigation before the two ICC judicial chambers could provide added opportunity to obstruct justice. In an effort to avoid this, while respecting the important interest that states and the prosecutor may have in appealing, an expedited system for appealing the decisions of the Pre-Trial Chamber to defer or not to defer should be established.

- **Recommendation 3: The decision on appeal should be made by a simple majority.**

Comment: In addition, the proposal for a supermajority or unanimous judicial decision before the ICC prosecutor would be empowered to override national proceedings sets too high a threshold. If states are concerned that the ICC might be swayed by emotions or political pressures, the solution is to have a stringent initial selection process for the ICC judges and prosecutor to ensure that individuals of only the highest caliber are selected. Thereafter, confidence must be placed in their integrity and professionalism rather than constructing excessively high procedural hurdles that pose too great a risk of impeding the effective functioning of the Court. As indicated in the latest text of Article 82[74](4), appellate confirmations of judgments require, and should require, only a simple majority.

Burden of proof

- **Recommendation: The state seeking deferral should bear the burden of proving that the investigation or prosecution on the national level are sufficient to justify deferral. This should apply also in the event of any**

appeal against the Pre-Trial Chamber's decision, by a state or the prosecutor.

Comment: The proposed Article *16[11 bis]* creates a strong presumption in favor of national proceedings and suggests that, in the event of a challenge to the sufficiency of national proceedings, the burden of proof would be on the ICC prosecutor to demonstrate their insufficiency. This would impose a potentially impossible burden on the prosecutor, as most of the relevant information about national proceedings would be in the hands of national authorities, not the ICC prosecutor. Instead, the burden of proof should be placed on the party best able to produce the relevant evidence: the state party. While the ICC prosecutor could fairly be expected to make a preliminary showing that there is reason to believe that national proceedings are insufficient, the crossing of that threshold should shift the burden of proof to the state party in question to demonstrate that its investigative and prosecutorial efforts remain vigorous and genuine.

Multiple challenges to admissibility on the basis of complementarity

- **Recommendation: Admissibility should be challenged by states only once. If the state challenges at this pre-investigative phase and loses, it should not, in general, be able to challenge again under Article 17[12]. The Court should be able to make an exception to this general rule.**

Comment: In the event that the ICC's Pre-Trial and Appeals Chambers uphold the prosecutor's decision to proceed, proposed Article *16[11 bis]* would enable the state to lodge further challenges to admissibility on the grounds of complementarity under Article 17[12]. Paragraph 5 of proposed Article *16[11 bis]* permits the state to have two opportunities to challenge admissibility, notwithstanding that this was clearly not envisioned by Article 17[12](3), which provides that a person or state may challenge admissibility only once.

Permitting multiple challenges to admissibility would unduly delay the prosecutor's ability to proceed with investigations and prosecutions, and potentially jeopardize the integrity of the evidence, as outlined above. While basic due process would require allowing an individual defendant to challenge admissibility post-indictment, particularly as he or she may not have had the opportunity to do so at an earlier stage, there is in general no need to give the state a second opportunity to raise the matter if it has already done so unsuccessfully at the investigative stage.

However, Article *16[11 bis]* should provide--as Article 17[12] does--that in exceptional circumstances, the Court may grant leave for a second challenge to be brought. This would cover the situation where substantial new facts are available, or where a challenge based on the investigation of a "situation" under Article *16[11 bis]* failed, but different considerations pertain in respect of the investigation of a particular "case" arising out of that situation. For example, it is conceivable that, in exceptional cases, a state may fail to satisfy the Court that it had met the relevant standard in its investigation of the situation as a whole, but be able to satisfy the Court that it has conducted genuine, thorough investigations in one particular case. The Court should be endowed with the flexibility to embrace these situations, while ensuring that multiple challenges based on the same facts cannot obstruct and delay the important work of the ICC.

SECTION F : GENERAL PRINCIPLES OF CRIMINAL LAW

AGE OF RESPONSIBILITY

Article 26

- *Recommendation:* **As stated in Section B, the ICC should have jurisdiction only over persons who have attained eighteen years of age at the time of the commission of the crime in question. Article 2,6 dealing with the age at which a person shall be deemed criminally responsible under the statute, is therefore unnecessary and should be deleted.**

STATUTE OF LIMITATION

Article 27

- *Recommendation:* **The statute should exclude any statute of limitation for the core crimes within the jurisdiction of the Court.**

Comment: The ICC must not allow for the prescription of the very serious crimes within its jurisdiction. The crimes in question are of such gravity that they do not prescribe as a matter of international law and the ICC statute should adhere to this legal principle.

The Convention on the Non-Applicability of Statutory Limitations to War Crimes and Crimes against Humanity[187] provides at Article 1 that there shall be no statutory limitation for war crimes[188], crimes against humanity, apartheid and genocide. The European Convention on the Non-Applicability of Statutory Limitations to Crimes against Humanity and War Crimes,[189] enumerates the same list of crimes but adds that "any other violation of a rule or custom of

---

[187] New York, 26 November 1968, 754 U.N.T.S. 7, Reprinted in ILM 68 (1969); Schindler/Toman 837

[188] The convention refers to war crimes as defined in the Charter of the Nuremberg International Military Tribunal and grave breaches of the Geneva Conventions

[189] Strasbourg, 25 January,1974 ETS 82, Reprinted in 13 ILM 540

85

international law which may hereafter be established and which the Contracting State concerned considers as being of a comparable nature...." shall likewise not be subject to statutory limitation.

Moreover, it should be clear that the existence of statutes of limitations on the national level should not have any effect on proceedings before the Court, on the basis that the Court must apply international law and international standards, consistent with the international nature of the crimes.

DEFENSES

Introduction
As stated in other contexts, the protection of the rights of the suspect or the accused must be unequivocally guaranteed throughout the statute. The right to prepare one's defense is a fundamental human right.[190] Inherent in the enjoyment of this right is knowledge of the defenses the Court will and will not consider. One consequence of not making the defenses explicit in the statute is the uncertainty it creates for the accused as to whether a particular defense is possible, which may in turn affect the plea tendered by the accused.[191] The

---

[190] The International Covenant on Civil and Political Rights (ICCPR) states in Article 14(3) that "in the determination of any criminal charge against him, everyone shall be entitled" to the minimum guarantees of being informed "promptly and in detail" of the nature of the charges, in a language they understand; of having adequate time and facilities to prepare their defense; of being tried without undue delay, in their presence and with legal assistance, including the free assistance of an interpreter, if need be; and of being able to examine, or have examined, the witnesses against them. Similar language is reflected in the Convention for the Protection of Human Rights and Fundamental Freedoms, Article 6(3), and in the American Convention on Human Rights, Article 8(2).

[191] This arose in the recent case before the ICTY, the case of Prosecutor v. Drazen Erdomovic, ICTY, IT-96-22, (1996). The statute of the ICTY does not enumerate possible defenses. Although the accused originally pled guilty, he did so having made statements claiming he committed the crimes in question under duress. An appeal of the conviction was lodged alleging that "the offenses were committed under duress and without the possibility of another moral choice...and on the grounds that he was not accountable for his acts...." The Appeals Chamber decided duress or coercion did not constitute a complete defense to the killing of innocent people by a soldier. The chamber decided, however, that in the circumstances the guilty plea was not informed and ordered that "the case must be remitted to a Trial Chamber...so that the Appellant may have the opportunity to replead in full knowledge of the nature of the charges and the consequences of his plea." This situation may have been avoided if the statute of the Tribunal had specified which defenses the

statute should therefore set out an extensive but non-exhaustive list of possible defenses.

Delegates are urged to keep firmly in focus, in considering applicable defenses, the need for uncompromising fairness to the accused, as expressed by one writer in the following terms:
"[F]airness requires giving due notice of what constitutes prohibited conduct and of what will happen if the line between permissible and prohibited conduct is crossed. Insofar as the object is to indicate where to draw the line, and therefore to provide a practical guide to permissible conduct, it would follow that the law should not only define offenses but also specify in advance the kind of justifications that will render otherwise prohibited conduct permissible."[192]

In this section, we present our recommendations on specific defenses, following the order in which they appear in the statute.

Article 30

*   *Recommendation 1:* **Mistake of fact or law should not be cited as a ground for excluding criminal responsibility.**

Comment: Mistake of fact should extinguish criminal responsibility only in so far as it negates the mental element in crime. As such, its inclusion within the statute as a defense is unnecessary, as it is already covered under the relevant *mens rea* provisions.

Mistake of law should also be excluded from possible defenses, given the extremely grave nature of the crimes within the Court's jurisdiction. While mistake of law is recognized in many systems as a defense to the commission of certain crimes,[193] rarely does it extinguish responsibility for crimes as egregious

---

Tribunal could consider and which it could not.

[192] See Edward Wise, "General Rules of Criminal Law," 25 Denver Journal International Law & Policy 313.

[193] These might be categorized as crimes which are "mala prohibita," r acts the criminality of which derive from particular laws, rather than "mala in se" which are criminal due to their inherent wrongfulness. See Michael L.Travers, Comment, *Mistake of Law in Mala Prohibita Crimes*, 1995, 62 University of Chicago Law Review 1316.

as those falling within the jurisdiction of the ICC. Option 1 of Article 30 seeks to reflect this distinction by allowing the exclusion "provided that the mistake is not inconsistent with the nature of the alleged crimes." However, in the light of the limited scope of the Court's jurisdiction over genocide, crimes against humanity and war crimes, mistake of fact or law should be considered inconsistent with the nature of all of these crimes. In addition to the practical evidentiary problems that would result from having to ascertain the subjective question of whether such a "mistake" was or was not made, to allow this defense would undermine the seriousness of the crimes in question. Option 2, without the text that currently appears in brackets, is therefore the preferred option.

Article 31(a): mental disease

- **Recommendation:** **Retain the defense of incapacitating mental disease or defect.**

Comment: This defense is widely established as a full defense in civil and common law systems alike, often expressed as the defense of insanity. This was implicitly recognized by the Report of the Secretary General to the Security Council upon submitting the draft statute of the International Criminal Tribunal for the Former Yugoslavia.[194] The current text of Article 31(1)(a) should be supported. This defines the defense as such a mental disease or defect which, at the time of the commission of the crime, destroyed the person's capacity either to appreciate the criminality of his or her conduct or conform that conduct to the requirements of the law.

Article 31(1)(b): involuntary intoxication

- **Recommendation 3:** **Retain the defense of involuntary intoxication that, at the time of the commission of the crime, destroyed the person's capacity either to appreciate the criminality of his or her conduct or conform that conduct to the requirements of the law.**

Comment: Intoxication *per se* should not constitute an absolute defense. Where the extent of the intoxication is such that the person remains able to control his

---

[194] The Report indicated that "*[t]he International Tribunal itself will have to decide on various personal defenses which may relieve a person of individual criminal responsibility, such as minimum age or mental incapacity, drawing upon general principles of law recognized by all nations.*"

or her actions and appreciate the wrongfulness of them, or where the state of intoxication was freely entered into, the person should remain criminally responsible. It is worth noting that in circumstances of forced intoxication which does constitute a defense for the person forcibly intoxicated, the person responsible for inducing the state of intoxication could, of course, be responsible for the consequences of so doing, depending on all the facts and circumstances of the case.

The meaning of "involuntary" in this context is problematic, particularly with regard to drug or alcohol addiction, but this should be a matter for interpretation by the Court rather than requiring specific definition in the statute itself.

Article 31(1)(c): self-defense or defense of others

• *Recommendation 4:* **Retain self-defense or defense of others as a defense. This should not include defense of property.**

Comment: Self-defense or defense of others should apply where the person acts reasonably to defend him or herself or another person from an imminent use of force, in so far as the force employed in defense is reasonable to avoid the harm feared and is proportional to it. A person should not be criminally responsible when he or she acts in self-defense or to defend others from an imminent attack, and in doing so uses only reasonable force to meet that objective. Generally, self-defense is understood to cover the situation in which a person uses force against the person responsible for posing the imminent threat. It would not therefore cover the situation where force is used by A against B in response to an imminent attack from C.[195] The imminence requirement is an essential element in this defense, which distinguishes it from a premeditated reprisal.

Article 31(1)(d): threat of death or imminent bodily harm

• *Recommendation 5:* **Retain as a defense the existence of a real and imminent threat of death or serious bodily harm, where the response to that threat did not cause greater harm than the one sought to be avoided. This should only apply where the person did not knowingly**

---

[195] Recommendation 4, following this comment, in respect of real and imminent threat of death or serious bodily harm.

expose him or herself to the threat. Protection of property should not be among the defenses.

Comment: This defense should be available in exceptional circumstances.[196] The existence of duress and coercion should not necessarily relieve an individual of criminal responsibility.[197] However, where all the components of the above definition are present, such that the only choice was to inflict or to suffer serious bodily injury or death, the Court should be able to decide that the person was not criminally responsible. This corresponds with the view adopted by the Nuremberg Tribunal that an individual is not required to "forfeit his life or suffer serious harm in order to avoid committing a crime which he condemns."[198] The evidentiary difficulties which may arise in establishing the existence of all of the components is undeniable, but this is, of course, a matter for evaluation by the Court in the light of all the evidence in a particular case. The inclusion of this provision is necessary to enable the Court to carry out that evaluation.

This defense should not apply to a person who knowingly exposes him or herself to the threat and then seeks to rely upon it as a defense for crimes committed. However, in the light of the reality of forced recruitment to armed forces,[199] and in particular the tragic and widespread recruitment of children,[200] we do not

---

[196] This is, we suggest, ensured by the above formulation which requires that the threat be real, serious and imminent, that the response must be proportional, and the person must not have knowingly exposed him or herself to the threat in question. See The United States v. Otto Ohlendorf, IV Trials of War Criminals Before the Nuremberg Military Tribunals Under Control Council Law No. 10, p. 411 (1950), hereinafter referred to as the "Einsatzgruppen judgment." The Nuremberg Tribunal in that case said that a threat that could absolve criminal responsibility had to be "imminent, real and inevitable."

[197] The existence of these factors short of satisfying the far higher threshold necessary for the purposes of this defense, may be taken into account as mitigating circumstances in sentencing, as set out in Section L on Penalties, below.

[198] Einsatzgruppen judgment, at p. 480.

[199] See, for example, Human Rights Watch/Americas, "Return to Violence: Refugees, Civil Patrollers, and Impunity," *A Human Rights Watch Short Report*, vol. 8, no. 1 (B), January 1996.

[200] See in particular, Human Rights Watch/Americas, "Return to Violence: Refugees, Civil Patrollers, and Impunity"; Human Rights Watch/Asia, "Burma: Children's Rights and the Rule of Law", *A Human Rights Watch Short Report*, vol 9. No 1, January 1997; Human Rights Watch/*Africa, Children of Sudan: Slaves, Street Children and Child Soldier,* (New York: Human Rights Watch, 1995); Human Rights Watch/Africa, *The Scars of Death: Children Abducted by the Lord's Resistance Army in Uganda* (New York, Human Rights Watch: 1997); Human Rights Watch, " Children In Combat," *A Human Rights Watch*

believe that it can be generally assumed that by virtue of being a "soldier" one has voluntarily exposed oneself to the threat in question.[201] Depending on the circumstances, this defense could apply to civilians or to members of armed forces.

This defense must be distinguished from the existence of superior orders as a defense which, as set out below, should be strongly opposed. While orders from superiors may in fact be coupled with the components set out above, such that the complete defense applies, the test "is not the existence of the order, but whether moral choice was in fact possible."[202]

Article 31 (c), (d), (e): the protection of property

- **Recommendation 6: Omit the protection of property as a defense.**

Comment: Defense of property should never constitute a full defense for crimes as egregious as those coming within the Court's jurisdiction. All references to property as a defense should therefore be deleted, in particular from Article 31(1), subparagraphs (c),(d),(e), where the reference now exists.

Article 32: Superior orders

- **Recommendation 7: Omit from the statute the defense of superior orders.**

Commentary: Superior orders must not constitute a defense to the crimes within the jurisdiction of the Court. Article 8 of the London Charter establishing the Nuremberg International Military Tribunal explicitly prohibited the application of superior orders as a defense, and this principle is by now well established in

---

Short Report, vol. 8, no. 1 (G), January 1996.
While Human Rights Watch opposes the ICC assuming jurisdiction over persons under the age of eighteen, many persons over eighteen at the time of the commission of the crime will have been forcibly recruited prior to that age.

[201] See, in this respect, the separate opinion of Judge McDonald and Judge Vohrah of the Appeals Chamber decision in Prosecutor v. Erdomovic, ICTY, IT-96-22-A, (7 October 1997). See above, Section F, on defenses.

[202] The judgments of the Nuremberg Tribunal considered the defense of superior orders where circumstances were such that the subordinate was deemed to have had no moral choice or alternative to carrying out the order.

international law.[203] The specific exclusion of superior orders as a defense is also expressed in international instruments such as the Convention against Torture and Other Inhuman or Degrading Treatment or Punishment.[204] The principle is reflected in Security Council Resolution 955 (1994) establishing the International Criminal Tribunal for Rwanda.[205] Consistent with the approach developed since the Nuremberg Tribunal, such orders may be taken into account as a mitigating factor in determining punishment, but do not exonerate criminal responsibility.[206]

Article 34: Other grounds for excluding criminal responsibility

• **Recommendation 10: The specified defenses should constitute a non-exhaustive list. The Court should be allowed to accept additional defenses to those specified in the statute, if it is satisfied that such defenses are enshrined in the principles of criminal law common to civilized nations.**

Comment: The enumeration of a list of defenses should be strongly supported, in the interests of protecting the rights of the defendant, but that list should be non-exhaustive. The bracketed text of Article 34(1)(a) which suggests that where a defense exists in the "[principles of criminal law common to civilized nations]" the ICC should be able to apply any such defense, should be supported. The application of national law, as envisaged by the other bracketed option ("[in the State with the most significant contacts to the crime]"), should be opposed on the basis of the disparity in the treatment of accused persons that would follow from

---

[203] In the trial of Adolf Eichmann, the Israeli district court observed that the rejection of the superior orders defense in the prosecution of war criminals had been acknowledged by the United Nations in 1946 and had "now become general in all civilized nations." A.G. of the Government of Israel v. Adolf Eichmann, (Dec. 12, 1961) 36 International Review 18, 20 (1968), at p. 257, affirmed Text of Judgment of the Supreme Court (May 29, 1962), p. 317-18. See also U.N.G.A. Res. 95(1).

[204] See Article 2(3).

[205] S/RES/955 (1994) November 8, 1994. Art. 6(4) of the statute of the International Criminal Tribunal for Rwanda states that "the fact that an accused person acted pursuant to an order of a Government or of a superior shall not relieve him or her of criminal responsibility, but may be considered in mitigation of punishment if the International Tribunal for Rwanda determines that justice so requires."

[206] The London Charter allowed for superior orders to constitute a mitigating factor but not a full defense. This was contrary to what most military laws provided for at the time World War II started.

it. The Court should however be empowered to apply a defense which it finds to be supported by general principles of law,[207] and able to look to general practice in national systems as a source from which to assess those principles. As the right of an accused person to present any relevant defense is a fundamental right which the statute must guarantee, the inclusion of this provision is important. Moreover, this provision would endow the Court with the necessary flexibility to respond to future developments in international law and principles.

---

[207] Article 38 of the statute of the International Court of Justice provides that general principles of law common to civilized nations is a source of international law applicable by that Court.

SECTION G: APPLICABLE LAW

Introduction:
Any discussion of the question of applicable law should be framed by the following guiding principles. The first is the principle of legality, encompassing the requirement of certainty as to the law. In accordance with this principle, the statute must set out the applicable law with the greatest possible degree of clarity. Secondly are the principles of equality and universality. As an international court charged with upholding international law, the Court must operate at all times consistent with that body of law. As such, all accused persons must be accorded equal treatment without discrimination on any basis.[208]

STATUTE AND INTERNATIONAL LAW

Article 20(1)

- ***Recommendation 1:*** **The ICC should apply the statute and rules of the Court and applicable international law, including general principles of law recognized by national legal systems. National laws may be taken in account as a relevant fact, not applied as binding law. As such, Option 1 in Article 14(1)(c)[209] should be retained and option 2 deleted[210].**

Comment: The statute must be the primary source of law for the Court. In the interpretation of the statute, the Court should have regard to the body of international law of which the statute is part. The ICC will be an international court with jurisdiction over crimes that offend the conscience of humankind, and over which there is universal jurisdiction. As such, and as a Court with a primary objective of enforcing international law, it is appropriate that the relevant standards to be applied by the Court are international.

---

[208] See, for example, Article 26 of the International Covenant on Civil and Political Rights (ICCPR), adopted December 16, 1966, (U.N. G.A. Resolution 2200 A XXI) 999 U.N.T.S. 171, which provides that "all persons are equal before the law and are entitled to the equal protection of the law. In this respect the law shall prohibit any discrimination, and guarantee to all persons the equal and effective protection against discrimination on any ground such as race, color, sex, language, religion or nationality...."

[209] In addition to applying treaties and the principles and rules of general international law, Option 1 allows the Court to apply "general principles of law derived by the Court from national laws of legal systems of the world." See comment below.

[210] Option 2 allows the Court to apply particular national laws

"General principles of law recognized by civilized nations" is one of the sources of international law, as established in Article 38 of the statute of the International Court of Justice.[211] As such, the reference in Article 20(1)(b) to "the principles and rules of general international law", already comprises the principles and rules of law generally recognized in national legal systems.[212] However, in the interest of clarity, specific reference could be made to these general principles of law as a source of applicable law.[213]

In the area of international criminal law, customary international and treaty law may not be sufficiently developed at the present time to provide legal guidance on all possible matters concerning the application of the statute.[214] General principles, derived from practice in a range of national legal systems, should be drawn upon to fill any potential *lacuna*.[215] The International Court of Justice has relied upon this source of law in the exercise of its judicial function,[216] as has the International Tribunal for the Former Yugoslavia.[217]

---

[211] Article 38(1)(c) of the Statute of the International Court of Justice, I.C.J. Acts and Documents, No 5 ("ICJ Statute").

[212] Referring to the general principles contained in Article 38(1)(c) of the ICJ statute, Lord McNair, then judge on the International Court of Justice, stated "[i]t is not the concrete manifestation of the principle in different national systems--which are anyhow likely to vary--but the general concept of law underlying them that the international judge is entitled to apply under paragraph (c)." *South West Africa case*, I.C.J.Rep(1950), p.148

[213]Such principles should apply in so far as consistent with the Statute and other sources of international law, as set out in the recommendation below.

[214] A paper submitted by the Canadian delegation to the 1996 Preparatory Committee, which Human Rights Watch supports, recognizes that on certain issues there is no developed body of international criminal law, such as on the question of applicable defenses, but that such a body is developing. This body of law will clearly continue to develop and guide the Court in the future.

[215] In the opinion of the Advisory Committee of Jurists on Article 38(1)(c) of the ICJ Statute, filling lacunae in treaties and customary international law was one of the objectives of including (c) within the sources of international law. Permanent Court of International Justice, Advisory Committee of Jurists, Proces verbaux of the Proceedings of the Committee (June 16-July 24 1920, L.N. Publication, 1920, p 335

[216] See the *North Sea Continental Shelf* case (Federal Republic of Germany v. Denmark and Federal Republic of Germany v. Netherlands - ICJ, 1969, 4) and the *Diversion of Water from the Meuse* case (Netherlands v. Belgium, PCIG, Ser. A/B, No. 70, 76-78. 4 Hudson, World Ct.Rep 172, 231-33).

[217] See for example, the recent case of *Prosecutor v. Drazen Erdomovic*, ICTY, IT-96-22-A, (1996), p 41.

Specific national laws, on the other hand, should never be a substitute for international law or general principles and directly applied by the ICC. It is widely accepted that the fact that a State does not criminalize genocide within its own legal system is not determinant of the Court's jurisdiction over nationals of that state who commit genocide. Similarly, other specific provisions of the national law of the state of nationality of the accused, or the state of the territory on which the crime was committed, should not be directly applied. National legal standards will inevitably vary; national laws may themselves be discriminatory or otherwise inconsistent with international law. Even where national laws are not incompatible with international law, we believe that an individual should not be treated more, or less, favorably in the prosecution of these crimes on the basis of his or her nationality.

PREVIOUS JUDICIAL DECISIONS

Article 20(2)

- *Recommendation*: **The Court should be able to apply the principles and rules of law as interpreted in its previous decisions, in line with the current wording of Article 20(2).**

Comment: The provision embodied in Article 20(2) would facilitate the cohesive development of the Court's jurisprudence, and contribute to the development of the emerging body of international criminal law. The current text of Article 20 does not propose establishing a system of binding legal precedent, or seek to oblige the Court to adhere to the terms of its earlier decisions. Rather, it is permissive, empowering the Court to do so. The Court's express ability to apply the principles that emerge from its previous judgments would contribute to greater consistency between cases and predictability, which are aspects of the principle of legality.

CONSISTENCY WITH INTERNATIONAL HUMAN RIGHTS LAW

Article 20(3)

- *Recommendation 2:* **Retain Article 20(3) as it now stands, making explicit that, "[t]he application and interpretation of law pursuant to this article must be consistent with internationally recognized human rights, which include the prohibition on any adverse distinction...."**

Comment: It will be essential to the ICC's credibility and legitimacy that the Court observe the highest standards of international human rights law. This affects many aspects of the statute, including the need for unequivocal respect for the rights of the accused and the duty of the Court to exercise its functions without adverse discrimination on the basis of gender, race or other grounds, as commonly defined by international human rights law.[218] The recent addition of this provision at the March/April Preparatory committee meeting enhances the current draft statute and should be retained.

---

[218] See for example, Article 26 of the ICCPR.

SECTION H: COMPOSITION AND ADMINISTRATION OF THE COURT

DIVERSITY IN THE COMPOSITION OF THE COURT

Article 37(8)(d)

- **Recommendation 1:** **States parties should take into account the need for gender balance in the composition of all organs of the Court, including the judiciary.**

Comment: The ICC will be better equipped to effectively discharge its mandate if its composition reflects gender balance. Judges will need to incorporate the perspectives of women when making critical decisions regarding the evaluation of evidence and the procedures for examining witnesses. The effective prosecution of gender-related crimes is an important challenge facing this Court. The possibility of successfully meeting this challenge will be greatly enhanced if women are included in the prosecutor's office, the Victim and Witness Unit, and the judiciary. "Gender balance" should be included as a factor for consideration in the election of judges and in the employment of the staff of the Registrar and the prosecutor, as currently proposed in Article 37(8)[30(5)](d).[219]

The constituent instruments of a number of international bodies make explicit reference to the importance of representation of women within these organizations.[220] Regard for gender balance in international bodies has been supported by the 1993 World Conference on Human Rights and the Fourth U.N. World Conference on Women in Beijing. Paragraph 43 of the Vienna Declaration and Programme of Action "...encourages other principal and subsidiary organs of the United Nations to guarantee the participation of women under conditions of equality."

- **Recommendation 2:** **States parties should take into account the need for the representation of the principal legal systems of the world and**

---

[219] While Article 37(8)[30(5)] sets out the factors to be taken into account in the election of judges, Article 45[37 bis] (2) provides that the criteria in Article 37(8)[30(5)] shall also apply to the employment of the staff of the Registrar and the prosecutor.

[220] See for example, Article 9(3) of the Constitution of the International Labor Organization which provides that "A certain number of the staff of the International Labor Office shall be women."

equitable geographical distribution in the election of the judges. The composition of all organs of the Court should be diverse, on the basis of race, national origin or ethnicity, among other factors.

Comment: Article 37(8)[30](5)](a) and (c) takes into account the representation of the principal legal systems of the world and equitable geographical distribution in the election of the judges. The ICC must be a universal court established to apply international law and the principles of law recognized in major legal systems.

The Court must have within its ranks persons of the highest standing, and should reflect a range of legal backgrounds and traditions--civil, common law and others. Uniformity of excellence, coupled with diversity on the basis set out in the recommendation above, would be an asset throughout the organs of the Court, not exclusively in the judiciary. Other parts of the Court, in particular the Procuracy and the Witness Support and Protection Unit of the Registry, would greatly benefit from an expert staff that was culturally diverse; this would facilitate sensitive and effective dealings with witnesses--in particular victims-- and accused persons.

LEGAL EXPERTISE IN SEXUAL AND GENDER VIOLENCE AND PROTECTION OF CHILDREN

• **Recommendation: States parties should take into account the need for legal expertise in sexual and gender violence and in the protection of children, in all organs of the Court, including the judiciary.**

Comment: Given the nature of the crimes which the Court will be prosecuting, all organs of the ICC would benefit greatly from legal expertise in sexual and gender violence and in the protection of children. Such experts should also be appointed in the office of the prosecutor, as proposed in Article 43[36](7), and in the staff of the Victims and Witness Unit.

Although Human Rights Watch has recommended that the Court should have no jurisdiction over persons who were under the age of eighteen at the time they are alleged to have committed a crime, the current draft statute leaves open the possibility that children might be prosecuted by the Court. In the unfortunate event that children may appear as defendants before the Court, we recommend that the Court have legal expertise not only on "violence against children," as envisioned in the current proposals, but on the protection of children generally. This would cover violence against children, the protection of children as witnesses and victims of crimes, and also the rights accorded to children as possible defendants under international juvenile justice standards.

VICTIM AND WITNESS SUPPORT AND PROTECTION UNIT

*   *Recommendation:* **A Victims and Witnesses Unit should be created within the Registry, operating independently of the Office of the Prosecutor.** **This unit will protect the physical and psychological well-being of victims, witnesses -- regardless of whether they are testifying for the defense or the prosecution --and their family members, before, during, and after trial proceedings.**

Comment: Providing support and protection to witnesses before, during, and after the trial phase is critical to the success of the ICC. Evidence from the International Criminal Tribunals for the Former Yugoslavia and Rwanda overwhelmingly indicate that witnesses face serious security, psychological, and other medical concerns. For example, numerous witnesses, in particular victims of gender-based crimes, have refused to participate in the tribunals' proceedings because of fears of reprisals against them or their families, or because of the social or familial ostracization that may result from having been a victim of a gender-based crime. Victims who do testify may experience profound stigma and shame. For these and other similar reasons, the Victims and Witnesses Unit must provide survivors with basic support and counseling services, in addition to protective measures, to promote their psychological well-being and facilitate their participation in ICC proceedings.

In the light of the unit's mandate, the unit should be located within the Registry of the Court, and not within the Procuracy. The prosecutor will and must be sensitive to the concerns of witnesses in the proper exercise of his or her functions. However, it is possible that conflict could develop between the interests of witnesses, on the one hand, and the interest of the prosecutor's office--in ensuring the effective prosecution of those responsible for serious crimes on the other. In their interventions in the March-April Preparatory Committee session, registrars from the International Criminal Tribunals for the Former Yugoslavia and Rwanda emphasized the "neutral role" of the Registry and supported the location of the Unit within the Registry.[221] To ensure that the

---

[221] "[T]he distinction between witnesses for the prosecutor and for the defense is irrelevant and could in some cases lead to inequitable results.... More often than not, the interest of a witness in securing his or her personal safety will not coincide with the interests

interests of the witnesses are adequately represented and protected, Human Rights Watch recommends that the unit operate independently from the prosecutor's office.

THE RULES OF PROCEDURE AND EVIDENCE

Article 52(1)

- *Recommendation:* **The Rules of Procedure and Evidence should be adopted separately from the statute for the Court.**

Comment: Option 2 of Article 52(1) proposes that the Rules of Procedure and Evidence shall enter into force together with the statute for the ICC. We believe that this proposal would inevitably delay the entry into force of the statute and the establishment of the ICC. The fundamental principles of procedure and evidence which will underlie the creation of the rules should be set forth in the statute, with the detailed manifestation of those principles left for the rules. Given that the ICC statute does in fact set out provisions relating to evidence and procedure with some precision, and that the rules must be drawn up in line with those principles enshrined in the statute, the concerns of those states that have argued that they must see the content of the rules in order to know what kind of Court they will be signing on to, are unfounded. Moreover, it should be borne in mind that the responsibility for drafting the rules, according to the statute, lies with the states parties themselves (as opposed to the judges who would have responsibility only for the internal regulations of the Court). Through ratification, therefore, states can ensure that they are closely involved in the process of creation of the Rules of Evidence and Procedure.[222]

---

of either party in protecting this witness. The interest of the latter will usually be limited to a witness's role in 'winning the case'. As in the case of the ICTY, it should therefore be the court which is entrusted with the protection of witnesses. Within the court, it is my position that only the Registry is sufficiently neutral to provide this protection. The Registry is therefore the most appropriate place for the location of a Witness Unit." Address of the Registrar of the International Criminal Tribunal for the former Yugoslavia Mrs. Dorothee de Sampayo Garrido-Nijgh to the Preparatory Committee on the Establishment of an International Criminal Court (March/April Session, 16 March - 3 April 1998, New York), 19 March 1998.

[222] The judges for the International Tribunals for the former Yugoslavia and Rwanda were responsible for drafting the Rules of Procedure and Evidence. See statutes of ICTY, Article 15; ICTR, Article 14.

Delegates are urged not to permit the process of elaboration of the detailed rules of procedure to jeopardize the timely establishment of this institution that the international community so urgently demands.

SECTION I: INVESTIGATION AND PROSECUTION

This section contains recommendations and comments on specific matter relating to the investigation and prosecution of cases before the ICC.

NOTIFICATION

Article 54(2)[47(1)bis]: Notification of states [parties] and informing named individuals

• **Recommendation: Delete the reference in Article 54(2)[47(1)*bis*] to states parties informing persons within their jurisdiction referred to in a submission to the Court that an investigation is about to commence. State parties should not, in general, inform such persons of an investigation to be initiated but should be obliged to treat as confidential the information provided by the Court.**

Comment: Article 54(2)[47(1)*bis*] provides that the prosecutor shall notify state parties of any complaint or decision of the Security Council prior to initiating an investigation and that the states shall so inform persons within their jurisdiction who are referred to by name in the submission.[223]

States must be informed of an investigation in order to have the opportunity to challenge the exercise of the Court's jurisdiction on the basis of complementarity. However, every effort must be taken to minimize the risk of destruction of evidence and intimidation of victims and witnesses. Measures designed to counter such risks are set out in the context of Article 54[47].

The current obligation on state parties to inform the persons, such as the suspect, who may be named in the submission should be strongly opposed, due to the obvious risk that the suspect will abscond. In practice it would severely reduce the prospect of bringing criminals to justice and may expose witnesses to risk. Rather, the state should be under an obligation not to disclose the relevant information to named individuals, unless requested to do so by the Court.

While there is logic behind the need to inform states, so that a right to challenge may be exercisable, there is no justification for informing suspects or others at

---

[223] To be consistent with the trigger mechanisms proposed above, this article should include reference to the decision to investigate *ex officio.*

this preliminary stage. Persons named in a submission to the Court as responsible for crimes within its jurisdiction are not necessarily persons who will be "suspects" within the meaning of the statute. At a certain stage a person suspected of a crime must be informed of this fact, for example prior to being questioned. This and other rights of suspects and accused persons are protected at various points in the statute, according to the highest standards of criminal justice.[224] Notification prior to investigation however, is not a right that should be protected, but rather is a threat which could seriously undermine the prospects of a successful investigation and which should be strongly opposed.

PRIORITIZING INVESTIGATIONS IN THE INTERESTS OF JUSTICE

Article 54(2)(b)(ii)bis[47(1 bis)(b)(ii)bis]: The prosecutor's power to prioritize as required by the interests of justice

- **Recommendation: Afford the prosecutor the flexibility to decide whether an investigation would be in the interests of justice in a particular case, taking into account the gravity of the offense.**

Comment: As the ICC will have jurisdiction only over very serious crimes, it is unlikely that the Court will be inundated with cases. It is, however, almost inevitable that at some stage it will be necessary for the prosecutor to prioritize complaints received. It is appropriate that he or she have the flexibility to do so, and to pursue the cases that are clearly most in the interests of justice, such as the more egregious over the less egregious crimes.

This does not, as certain delegates suggested during the August Preparatory Committee meeting, give the prosecutor unbridled discretion to pick and chose between cases. Any decision to pursue a case would of course be subject to the approval of the Pre-Trial Chamber of the Court under new Article 12[46], just as a decision of the prosecutor not to pursue an investigation would, under Article 54(8)[47(5)], also be subject to review by the Court.[225] The power of any prosecutor, domestic or international, to prioritize his or her caseload is essential to the efficient conduct of investigations and to ensure the prosecution of the most serious crimes without delay.

---

[224] See Article 54(10)[47(6)(a)] of the statute.
[225] Article 54(8)[47(5)] refers to review by the Presidency or Pre-Trial Chamber.

Moreover, the inclusion of this provision should adequately address the concern about the potential overloading of the court preventing it from being able to function. Finally, it should quash any suggestion that a threshold limiting the court's jurisdiction to crimes committed pursuant to a plan or policy is necessary to ensure that the Court can prosecute the most serious crimes.[226]

ON-SITE INVESTIGATIONS

Article 54(4)[47](2): The prosecutor's power to conduct on-site investigations

- *Recommendation:* **The statute must enable the prosecutor to conduct on site investigations without requiring the consent of any state party.**

Comment: Article 54(4)(c)[47](2)(c)] provides various options in respect of the power to conduct on-site investigations and the consent that one of those options proposes as a pre-requisite for the exercise of that power. The power to conduct such investigations will be essential for the proper investigation of the crimes in question, and for the Court to satisfy itself that information on which it is basing its case is reliable. As such it go to the heart of ensuring fair prosecutions. Even in circumstances where the state is cooperating fully with the Court in the gathering of evidence, on-site investigations will nonetheless be important. The prosecutor, as the person responsible for the investigation, is best placed to know the necessary scope of the investigation and nature of evidence sought in the particular case.

The consent of states parties must not be a pre-requisite to an on-site investigation. State parties should not be able to withhold consent and hamper the prosecutor's ability to execute one of essential steps in an investigation. Under Part 9 of the statute,[227] state parties have a clear duty to cooperate with the investigation and prosecution of crimes within the jurisdiction of the Court. Requiring their consent implies that there is not such an obligation.[228]

---

[226] See Section A, Part 1 of this document on the definition of war crimes to come within the jurisdiction of the Court.

[227] See comment at Section N of this document.

[228] Article 85[77] and 86[78] of Part 9 of the statute set out the states' duty to cooperate with the Court.

Pre-Trial chamber's ability to review the decision of the prosecutor to carry out an on-site investigation,[229] in accordance with Option 2(ii) of 54(4)(c)[47](2)(c)], would safeguard against any possible abuse by the prosecutor of the power to conduct on-site investigations. While in fulfilment of its investigatory mandate the prosecutor's office may be subject to judicial review, it should not be dependant on the consent of any state party, neither as to whether nor when an onsite visit takes place. States should not be able to cause delay, and create opportunities for the flight of suspects or destruction of evidence. Should they do so, there should be no question as to their failure to meet their treaty obligations.

Consistent with the territorial sovereignty of the state, the prosecutor would, in general, be required to seek the consent of non-state parties in order to enter on their territory.[230] Any provision in this context relating to state consent should therefore relate only to non state parties.

THE PRESERVATION OF EVIDENCE

Article 54[47]: The preservation of evidence

• *Recommendation:* **Support the inclusion of a provision in this part empowering a prosecutor to take measures to preserve evidence, as may prove necessary for the effective conduct of ICC proceedings. This power should be available at any stage of the investigation, or where the prosecutor has deferred or suspended investigation in accordance with the statute.**

Comment: The prosecutor should have the power to preserve evidence as may prove necessary for the conduct of an effective ICC prosecution. The prosecutor must ensure that where it may be necessary to conduct ICC prosecution in the future, sufficient and reliable evidence will be available to do so.[231] In this

---

[229] Such a power could be added to the functions specified under 57[50](2), as set out at the relevant section below.

[230] This would not apply where the referral was by virtue of a decision of the Security Council.

[231] We made arguments to this effect in the context of Article *16[11 bis]*, but believe it would appropriate to include this important power in the context of Article 54[47] relating to the investigative powers of the prosecutor.

respect, we support the proposal submitted by one delegation,[232] made in the context of Article 54(3)[47](1)*ter,* to the effect that where the prosecutor defers to national investigations, he or she should be able to take measures to preserve evidence. This provision would operate in the circumstances to which Article 55[48] and 56 [49] relate[233] as well as *16[11 bis]*, and potentially in other circumstances where the Court's jurisdiction is suspended.[234]

The prosecutor would not take such a measure as a matter of course but only if it appears necessary, for example to prevent evidence being destroyed, lost or tampered with, or where testimony may no longer be available or reliable in the absence of the measures. To provide assurance against the improper use of this power, the Pre-Trial Chamber would review any decision by the prosecutor to take such measures, as provided for in Article 57[50](2)(iii).

INFORMATION REGARDING NATIONAL PROCEEDINGS

Article 55[48]: Information on national proceedings

• **Recommendation: States parties should promptly inform the prosecutor about national investigations or proceedings undertaken with respect to the alleged commission of a crime within the jurisdiction of the Court.**

Comment: Consistent with the general duty to cooperate with the Court, and the fact that the ICC may often be in position to assist national investigations into the crimes within its jurisdiction, state parties should share information with the ICC in relation to investigations covered by the scope of this article. Article 55[48] complements the provisions of Article 15[11] and Article 17[12] which frame the situations where the Court may exercise its jurisdiction in lieu of a national system that is unwilling or unable to effectively pursue prosecutions. In order to enable to the Court to do this, states should be obliged to provide information to the prosecutor, so that he or she (or, in the event of challenge, the

---

[232] See the proposal submitted to the March/April Preparatory Committee on 27 March 1998 by the delegation of France, A/AC249/1998/WG.4/DP37. The proposal related to Article 54(3) [47](1)*ter.*

[233] See recommendations on Article 56 [49] in the following section on information concerning national proceedings

[234] Human Rights Watch opposes the power of the Security Council to suspend an investigation as set out in the context of our commentary on Article 10. However, if the statute were to provide for circumstances in which such suspension of the Court's jurisdiction would occur, this provision on the preservation of evidence should operate.

Court) will be able to determine whether there are, in fact, genuine national proceedings and, if so, defer to the national jurisdiction. In order for the Court to determine whether its jurisdiction should be activated, on the basis that the national jurisdiction is "unable" or "unwilling" to effectively carry out investigation and prosecution, it must be able to obtain adequate information relating to national proceedings and should be supported. Where the information as to such investigations and prosecutions points to an absence of genuine proceedings, the prosecutor must be empowered to take up the matter. Should a state object to the ICC exercising its jurisdiction, there are adequate mechanisms for challenging the exercise of jurisdiction as set forth at Article 17[12] of the statute.

Article 56[49]: Deferral of an investigation by the prosecutor

• **Recommendation:** **Support the inclusion of a provision to the effect that, where the prosecutor defers an investigation on the grounds of complementarity, states must make available to the prosecutor information on the proceedings to enable the prosecutor to determine whether the standard of complementarity is in fact being met by those proceedings. The above article should be amended to specify the state's obligation to provide all relevant information without delay.**

Comment: The prosecutor must be empowered to obtain information on the ongoing status of national proceedings where, regarding a potential investigation or prosecution, an initial decision has been made to defer to national authorities. The provision as presently drafted refers to a "request" to the state but does not make clear the obligation on the state to comply with such a request. The wording of Article 56[49] should be imperative, making clear that the state shall provide the information in response to such a request. This is consistent with the general duty to cooperate fully with the Court in Article 85[77].

As in Article 55[48], some reference should be made to the nature of the information to be provided; it should, as in the previous article, be sufficiently full as to progress made in the investigation and prosecution of the case, to enable the prosecutor to decide whether there are genuine proceedings that meet the Article 15[11] threshold. If, in light of the information provided, the prosecutor decides that the ICC should proceed with the case, the state should be notified. Sufficient safeguards then exist in the draft statute at Article 17[12] for relevant states to challenge this exercise of jurisdiction by the Court if they wish to do so.[235]

ORDERS

Article 57[50]

* **Recommendation: The statute should clarify that the Pre-Trial Chamber has the authority to issue subpoenas and to make other orders relating to the investigation, and that such orders are binding upon state parties.**

Comment: Article 57[50](2) provides a nonexhaustive list of the measures that the Pre-Trial Chamber may take to facilitate investigation and to protect the rights of the suspects. In the interests of clarity and consistency, this list should correspond with the powers of the Pre-Trial Chamber set out elsewhere in the statute. For example, Article 57 should include the power to issue subpoenas, as provided for in Article 54(4)[47(2)].

State cooperation in the enforcement of orders will be essential. Part IX of the statute deals only with state cooperation and compliance with requests from the Court, and Part X deals with enforcement of the judgments of the Court. The current draft statute does not address the critical question of cooperation in the enforcement of orders, such as subpoenas. Therefore, Article 57 should fill this gap, and clarify that orders of the Pre-Trial Chamber issued under this article are binding upon state parties.

Articles 58 to 61

During the March-April 1998 Preparatory Committee session, a proposal for an alternate text to Articles 51 to 54 of the Zutphen text (Article 58 to 61 of the current text) was proposed by several states.[236] This document was incorporated into the April 14, 1998 consolidated text of the draft statute[237] as a "Further Option for Articles 58 to 61" (hereinafter "the Further Option"). The general approach of the Further Option, which vests authority over most preliminary matters in the Pre-Trial Chamber, as opposed to the Presidency, should be supported. Decisions regarding the indictment confirmation, arrest, detention,

---

[235] See Article 17[12] "Challenges to jurisdiction."
[236] This proposal was issued in document A/AC.249/1998/WG.4/DP.40.
[237] A/Conf.183/2/Add.1.

interim release, and pretrial orders will have a significant impact on the basic rights of defendants. Accordingly, it is more appropriate for such decisions to be made by a collegiate body, exercising judicial functions, than by the Presidency.

The following recommendations and comments are offered on specific provisions of the consolidated text and, where appropriate, the Further Option. Citations of Articles 58 - 61 [51 - 54] generally relate to the consolidated text, except where otherwise indicated.

CONFIRMATION OF INDICTMENTS

Article 58[51](2)

• **Recommendation: The standard for confirming indictments should not impose an unreasonable burden on the Prosecutor. Determining the existence of a "prima facie" case, or that there is "sufficient evidence to establish substantial grounds to believe that the person committed each of the crimes charged" are more appropriate than requiring the Pre-Trial Chamber to determine that "there is sufficient evidence that could justify a conviction of a suspect, if the evidence were not contradicted at trial," as contained in the current consolidated text.**

Comment: Making confirmation of the indictment dependant on the prosecutor's ability to demonstrate "sufficient evidence that could justify a conviction of a suspect, if the evidence were not contradicted at trial" requires the prosecutor to establish the guilt of the suspect, even before all the witnesses have been interviewed and all the evidence has been collected. This standard would essentially call upon the Pre-Trial Chamber to make a preliminary judgment of the guilt of the person in question, and could bring into question the pre-judgment of the case by the Court.

The statutes for the International Tribunals for the former Yugoslavia and Rwanda provide that indictments shall be confirmed if the prosecutor has established a prima facie case.[238] The standard contemplated by the Further Option requires "sufficient evidence to establish substantial grounds to believe that the person committed each of the crimes charged." These standards would

---

[238] Statute of the ICTY (Article 98), ICTR (Article 18).

be sufficiently rigorous to protect the suspect from groundless charges, while imposing a reasonable burden on the prosecutor.

ORDERS REGARDING THE CONDUCT OF TRIAL

Article 58(10)[51(5)]

- *Recommendation*: **The current text should be retained, authorizing the Pre-Trial Chamber to make orders regarding the conduct of the trial "including, inter alia, orders requiring the disclosure of evidence to the defense, or providing for the protection of the accused, victims, witnesses, and confidential information."**

Comment: Article 58(10) authorizes the Pre-Trial Chamber to make orders regarding important measures that would ensure fairness and due process in the conduct of the trial, including compelling the disclosure of evidence to the defense and providing for the protection and privacy of the accused, victims, and witnesses.[239] The Further Option to Articles 58 - 61 omits this provision which should be included in the final text of the statute.

- *Recommendation*: **The statute should recognize the prosecutor's duty to disclose relevant evidence to the defense while permitting the Court to review the disclosure and make appropriate orders.**

Comment: The protection of the right of the accused to an adequate defense requires statutory recognition that the prosecutor has a *duty* to disclose all relevant evidence to the accused. As presently drafted, the Court *may* make an order as to disclosure. The statute should clarify that whether or not such an order is made, all information of potential relevance to the preparation of a defense must be made available to the accused. However, only potentially *relevant* evidence should have to be disclosed to the accused. To impose an obligation on the prosecutor to reveal *all* evidence gathered in the course of a complex investigation would be simply unworkable.

The proposal in Article 58(1)[51(5)] to empower the Pre-Trial Chamber to review disclosure, acting either on its own initiative or at the request of either party, should be supported. Such review may lead to an order by the Pre-Trial

---

[239] Note that Article 57[50], which also refers to orders by the Pre-Trial Chamber, relates only to those orders that have bearing on the investigation.

Chamber that the Prosecutor disclose further evidence to the defense. However, giving due consideration to the safety and privacy of witnesses and victims, the Pre-Trial Chamber should also be able to order the redaction of information (including the identity and whereabouts of victims and witnesses), when such information is unnecessary for the preparation of a defendant's case and its disclosure would jeopardize the security and well-being of individuals.

PRE-TRIAL ARREST AND DETENTION

Article 59[52](2)

• **Recommendation: Any detention without charge should be as short as possible, and subject to a maximum period. The statute should be amended to explicitly provide that the suspect has a right to be released if she or he is not charged within the specified time period.**

Comment: Article 9(2) of the ICCPR establishes "[a]nyone who is arrested shall be...promptly informed of any charges against him." When a suspect has not even been charged with a crime, there should therefore be very strict limitations on the period of pre-indictment detention, and the extension of such detention should be permitted only under exceptional circumstances.

A maximum time period should therefore be established, within which the indictment must be confirmed, as set forth in the current draft of Article 59[52](2). This time period should be kept as short as practicably possible. The restriction contained in Article 52(2), which permits the Pre-Trial Chamber to extend the period of pre-indictment detention only under exceptional circumstances and subject to strict time limits, is a valuable addition to the text.

The current draft statute fails, however, to specify that the suspect must be released upon the expiry of the relevant period, and given the importance of the rights concerned, this defect should be remedied.

ISSUING AN INTERNATIONAL ARREST WARRANT

Article 59(4)

• **Recommendation: The Pre-Trial Chamber should have the power to take appropriate measures when an arrest warrant, issued under Article 59, has not been executed. Specifically, such measures should include the issuance of an international warrant for the arrest of the** accused,[240] delivered to all states and binding on state parties, or ordering the freezing of assets of the accused without prejudice to the rights of third parties. Where the prosecutor satisfies the Court that the failure to execute a warrant was due to the failure of a state party to cooperate with the Tribunal, the Court may so communicate to other state parties.[241]

Comment: The Court must develop a mechanism towards ensuring that accused persons cannot escape conviction by absconding or otherwise refusing to submit to the jurisdiction of the Court. The Court should be empowered to insist that all state parties share responsibility for bringing to trial those indicted by the Court. The adoption of this recommendation would mean that, in the event of an accused person being shielded from prosecution by the State on whose territory she or he is residing, the accused could be arrested on entering the territory of another state party to the treaty, or cooperative non-state party.

INTERIM RELEASE

Article 60(4),(7)[53(3),(6)]

* *Recommendation*: **Applications for interim release should be determined by the Pre-Trial Chamber, not national judicial authorities. The provision allowing appeals of determinations regarding release or detention should be retained.**

Comment: The current text of Article 60(4) contains bracketed options allowing either national authorities or the Pre-Trial Chamber to determine whether a person should be released pending transfer to the Court. Attributing this role to national judicial authorities would undermine the authority of the Court on the crucial questions relating to the conduct of its proceedings. Competence over the interpretation and application of this statute should be vested solely in the Court, and, therefore, any reexamination of the criteria in Article 59[52](1) justifying arrest should be the responsibility of an organ of the Court, such as the Pre-Trial Chamber, rather than a national judicial authority.

---

[240] This procedure was adopted by the International Criminal Tribunal for the Former Yugoslavia in Rule 61(d) and invoked by the Trial Chambers I and II in several cases.

[241] The Statute of the Tribunal for the former Yugoslavia, in Rule 61 (A), (B), (D) and (E), contains provisions similar, though not identical, to those proposed above.

The Court must be committed to protecting personal liberty and providing mechanisms for full due process to ensure that any deprivation of liberty is justified. The Pre-Trial Chamber's decisions regarding detention and release, including decisions on applications for interim release either prior to or following transfer, must therefore be subject to appeal by either party, as provided for in Article 60(7)[53(6)]. The Further Option to Articles 58 - 61 does not contain any comparable provision. Delegates are urged to ensure the inclusion of a right to appeal this important decision.

PERIOD OF PRE-TRIAL DETENTION

Article 60(7)[53(6)](b)

• **Recommendation: The statute should contain strict restrictions on pretrial detention. What constitutes a reasonable period of pretrial detention will vary depending on the nature of the particular case, but should be subject to a maximum period. The Court should only grant extensions of detention under exceptional circumstances, and for good reason.**

Comment: Consistent with the fundamental nature of the right to liberty and security of the person, and of the presumption of innocence, pretrial detention should occur only exceptionally, and must be restricted.[242] The accused can only be held for a "reasonable time"[243] pending trial, or she or he has the right to be released. While a determination of what constitutes a "reasonable" period of detention can only be made on upon full consideration of the particular circumstances of each case, and will vary from case to case we believe that setting a maximum period of detention is essential to protect the interests of the accused.[244]

---

[242] Article 9(3) the ICCPR states that "Anyone arrested or detained on a criminal charge shall be brought promptly before a judge or other officer authorized by law to exercise judicial power and shall be entitled to trial within a reasonable time or release pending trial. It shall not be the general rule that persons awaiting trial shall be detained in custody." The Human Rights Committee has interpreted this as the right to a trial which produces a final judgment without undue delay (Adolfo Drescher Caldas v. Uruguay (43/1979) Selected Decisions, vol.2 at p. 81).

[243]Ibid.

[244]The Human Rights Committee has indicated on one occasion that a six month period from the date of detention to the conclusion of the trial may violate the Covenant. See the Report of the Forty-fifth Session Supplement no.40 (A/45/40), para 47, concerning

For these reasons, the formulation in Article 60(7)[53(6)](b) which sets a maximum period for detention and permits an extension only upon a demonstration of good cause for the delay by the prosecutor, and subject to an absolute maximum. The initial period of one year does, however, appear excessive. The Further Option to Article 60(4), which addresses restrictions on pretrial detention, is vaguely formulated and fails to establish a maximum period for detention.[245]

NOTIFICATION OF INDICTMENT

Article 61(2) [54(1 bis)]

* **Recommendation:** **The provision allowing for nondisclosure of indictments in extraordinary circumstances should be retained.**

Comment:
The Court should adhere to the principle of transparency in judicial proceedings to the greatest extent possible. However, extraordinary circumstances may call for the sealing of indictments, such as when public disclosure of the indictment is likely to prompt the flight of the accused, or pose a threat to victims and witnesses. Rule 53 of the Rules of Procedure and Evidence for the ICTY allows for the non-disclosure of evidence if it is "required to give effect to a provision of the Rules, to protect confidential information obtained by the Prosecutor, or is otherwise in the interests of justice."

Proposed Article 61(2) appropriately gives authority to the Pre-Trial Chamber to order the nondisclosure of indictments under specified conditions. Detailed provision may be included in the Rules, provided the statute reflects the principle that sealed indictments are permissible, albeit in exceptional circumstances.

---

pretrial detention in Democratic Yemen.
    [245]The Further Option to Article 60(4) reads as follows: "The Pre-Trial Chamber shall assure that a person is not detained for an unreasonable period prior to trial due to unexcusable delay by the Prosecutor. If such delay has occurred, the Court shall consider releasing the person pursuant to conditions."

SECTION J: THE TRIAL

In this section we address various important issues relating to the conduct of the trial, covered in Part VI of the statute.

SIGNIFICANCE OF A GUILTY PLEA

Article 65[58]: Proceedings on an admission of guilt

- *Recommendation 1*: **The statute should specify the responsibility of the Trial Chamber, upon receiving a guilty plea, to satisfy itself that such a plea was given freely and knowingly and is supported by the evidence available to the Court. The provision of Article 65[58] should therefore be retained.**

Comment: Article 65[58] is crucial in safeguarding the defendant from the consequences of mistakenly pleading guilty or from doing so as a result of coercion or other forms of external pressure[246]. We support the approach in paragraph (3) of allowing the Court the discretion to decide whether, taking into account all the circumstances of the case, the interests of justice demand that the Court proceed as if the guilty plea had not been tendered. Where the Trial Chamber is not so satisfied, it should request further information and/or, in exceptional circumstances where the interests of justice so demand, order that the trial proceed as if the guilty plea had not been rendered.

TRIALS IN ABSENTIA

Article 63[56]

- *Recommendation 1*: **Trials should not take place in the absence of the accused, and option 1 of Article 63[56] should therefore be retained.**

---

[246] This recommendation supports the original ILC Commentary to Article 38 which stated that following a guilty plea "[The Court] must at a minimum hear an account from the Prosecutor of the case against the accused and ensure for itself that the guilty plea was freely entered and is reliable." We believe that this merits explicit inclusion in the statute.

Comment: Trials in absentia should be prohibited on the basis that they jeopardize the rights of defendants and undermine the credibility of the Court. The ICC must operate according to the highest standards of international justice. This entails respect for a defendant's established legal right, inter alia, to be present during the trial,[247] to defend him/herself in person or through counsel of the defendant's choice,[248] to examine witnesses against them and to obtain the attendance and examination of witnesses in their support.[249]

While there is not an absolute prohibition on trials in absentia under international law,[250] there is a widespread perception that trials in absentia should not be provided for in the statute as they undermine the rights referred to above, as provided for in article 14 of the International Covenant on Civil and Political Rights.[251]

The statutes of the International Criminal Tribunals for the former Yugoslavia and Rwanda provide that the "accused shall be entitled...to be tried in his presence."[252] The Report of the Secretary-General Pursuant to Paragraph 2 of Security Council Resolution 808 notes that "a trial should not commence until the accused is physically present before the International Tribunal. In order to gain the legitimacy which is essential for the discharge of its mandate, the Court should similarly refrain from adopting procedures which may put in jeopardy the protection of the basic legal rights of the accused.

The court should, however, be able to take necessary measures to preserve evidence to ensure that a subsequent trial in the presence of the accused is possible.

---

[247] Article 14(3)(d) of the International Covenant on Civil and Political Rights ("ICCPR").

[248] Article 14(3)(d) of the ICCPR, Article 6(3)(c) of the European Convention on Human Rights ("ECHR"), and Article 8(2)(d) of the American Convention on Human Rights ("ACHR").

[249] Article 14(3)(e) of the ICCPR, Article 6(3)(d) of the ECHR, and Article 8(2)(f) of the ACHR.

[250] See the cases of Conteris v. Uruguay (Report, Op. Cit., para 1.5) and Colozza v Italy (1985) 7 EHRR 516 (Series A, No 89; Application No 9024/80), in the particular context of which trials *in absentia* were deemed violations of the relevant international law. It is acknowledged that the Human Rights Committee, for example, has expressed the view that trials *in absentia* are permissible when the accused has been informed of proceedings and declined to exercise his or her right to be present. Mbenge v. Zaire (UN Doc.A/37/40)

[251] Report of the Secretary-General Pursuant to Paragraph 2 of Security Council Resolution 808 (UN Doc S/25704), para. 101.

[252] See ICTY Statute, Article 21(4)(d) and ICTR Statute, Article 20(4)(d).

PROTECTION OF VICTIMS AND WITNESSES

Article 68[61]:

• ` *Recommendation:* Retain the Court's duty to protect the confidentiality[253] of witnesses and to take other appropriate measures, provided that such measures are consistent with the rights of the accused. The Court's consideration of whether to grant such protective measures should take place in camera at the request of either party, of the victim or witness concerned, of the Victims and Witnesses Unit, or *proprio motu,* at any time prior to or during the course of the trial. The parties should have the right to appeal decisions regarding confidentiality.

Comment: Full public access to information regarding ICC proceedings - including information regarding the identities of the participants involved in ICC proceedings -constitutes an important safeguard against injustice.[254] However, the Court must take into account genuine concerns for the physical and psychological well-being of witnesses and, in certain exceptional circumstances, grant some degree of confidentiality to protect witnesses and their families from reprisals and to shield them from the stigmatizing effect of public exposure.[255] Granting both parties the

---

[253] For purposes of this document, confidentiality refers to the non-disclosure of the victim's or witness' identity to the public or media, achieved by such measures as: the removal of names and identifying information from public records; non-disclosure to the public of any records identifying the victim; the restriction of photographs, sketches, video or audio recording in the precincts of the courtroom; the use of image- or voice-altering devices or closed-circuit television; and the assignment of pseudonyms.

[254] Note that while confidentiality can restrict access to or publication of a narrow range of identifying features - name, address, telephone number and photograph - it does not interfere with the press' ability to report fully and accurately the proceedings.

[255] The risk of retaliation against witnesses and their relatives on the part of accused persons or their supporters hardly needs to be stated. It is important to note that members of the government, military officers, and others with access to weapons and other means of reprisals or punishment are among the accused. Therefore, public testimony not only endangers the physical safety of witnesses and their family members, but also their job security, pension, housing, and ability to travel. Survivors of sexual violence can be particularly vulnerable to stigmatization. Sexual assault victims can be tainted as ineligible for marriage, or can risk divorce by their husbands, repudiation by their families, and ostracization by their communities. In light of prevailing cultural customs that condemn open discussion of sexual matters, many women can also experience profound shame and humiliation in testifying about their experiences before strangers. The use of screens and

right to appeal decisions regarding confidentiality will help to ensure that the highest standards of fairness are met.

*   ***Recommendation*: In instances where the Court grants confidentiality, the accused, the prosecutor, and state parties should be strictly prohibited from violating its order by releasing confidential information to the press or public. This should include direct and indirect identification of witnesses.**

Comment: Releasing information to the public or press can be devastatingly harmful to the physical and psychological welfare of witnesses. Moreover, it can discourage potential witnesses from coming forward to testify. The ICC should firmly censure disclosure of information in violation of its orders.

Article 68[61](9)

*   ***Recommendation*: Support the ability of states to seek protective measures from the Court to protect the life or physical integrity of their agents and servants. The protection of sensitive information, to which this article also relates, can be provided for in the freestanding article on the protection of national security.**

Comment: Comments on this Article are addressed in the section relating to the protection of national security interests, Section M. States should be entitled to seek measures to protect the life and safety of its agents. The protection on sensitive information should be subject to the criteria set out in the freestanding article on national security.

EVIDENCE

Article 69 [62]

*   ***Recommendation 1:* In the provisions relating to the giving of testimony to the Court, an appropriate balance must be struck between the interests of victim and witness protection on the one hand, and the rights of the accused on the other. In particular, the right to cross-examination of witnesses should be protected. This should be coupled with the addition**

---

other protective mechanisms to shield witnesses from the public during the course of trial can help secure their emotional and psychological well-being.

of a provision granting judges the discretion to control the manner of questioning, to avoid any harassment or intimidation of witnesses, or to prevent unnecessary trauma on their part.[256]

Comment: The statute appropriately recognizes the need for protective measures in favor of witnesses, particularly victims, while providing that such measures must not compromise the rights of the accused.[257] The adoption of such procedures should be supported with a view toward reducing the trauma of victims and witnesses, including minimizing the frequency with which victims must recount the atrocities committed against them.[258]

However, one of the "rights of the accused" which must not be compromised in any circumstances, is the right to cross-examination in person. This right is one of the minimum guarantees of the right to a fair trial enshrined in international instruments.[259] Article 67[60] of the statute, entitled "the rights of the accused," reflects the relevant international legal provisions, providing that the accused shall be entitled "to examine, or have examined, the prosecution witnesses and to obtain the attendance and examination of witnesses for the defense under the same conditions as witnesses for the prosecution."[260] It would be appropriate for the provisions of the statute relating to evidence to explicitly clarify that the right to cross examination cannot be compromised.[261]

---

[256] This recommendation is consistent with Rule 95 c) proposed by Australia and The Netherlands, as well as Rule 75 c)of both ad hoc tribunals. Both rules state, in relevant part: A Trial Chamber shall, whenever necessary, control the manner of questioning to avoid any harassment or intimidation.

[257] Article 68[61](1) states "The Court shall take the necessary measures available to it to protect the accused, victims and witnesses... [and] may, to that end, conduct closed proceedings or allow the presentation of evidence by electronic or other special means."

[258] This could be particularly important to protect victims of sexual violence. Recent history testifies to the frequency with which rape and other sexual violence is used as a weapon of war. Given the consequent likelihood that mass or successive rapes may come before the ICC, witnesses may have to testify, with traumatic results, against numerous defendants in the same or separate proceedings.

[259] For example, Article 14(3)(e) of the International Covenant on Civil and Political Rights, Article 6(3)(d) of the European Convention for the Protection of Human Rights and Fundamental Freedoms, and Article 8(2)(f) of the American Convention on Human Rights.

[260] Article 67[60](1)(e).

[261] Article 69 (evidence) currently provides for the giving of testimony in person, subject to protective measures taken under Article 68 (protection of victims, witnesses and the accused). Article 68 in turn states that those measures will not compromise the "rights

The Court should protect witnesses, particularly victims, from hostile cross-examination and innuendo during the course of trial. This is particularly important to protect victims of sexual violence from intimidating questions. It is important to grant judges discretion to admit witnesses' direct testimony against all similarly situated defendants. For example, given the likelihood that cases involving successive rapes may come before the ICC, witnesses may have to testify against numerous defendants in the same or separate proceedings. The ICC should adopt procedures with a view toward reducing the trauma of victims and witnesses, including minimizing the frequency with which victims must recount the atrocities committed against them. Judicial discretion to admit witnesses' direct testimony in subsequent proceedings should not, however, infringe on the accused's ability to cross-examine these witnesses or the ability of either party to elicit new testimony.

---

of the accused." The right to cross-examination is one such right, protected in the statute, at Article 67 (rights of accused). As such, the right to cross-examination may already be protected by the current draft. However, its protection would be more secure if were made clear in Article 69 that this right must not be compromised, or if Article 68 made explicit that the rights of the accused to which it refers are those enshrined in Article 67 and in international human rights instruments.

SECTION K: REPARATION TO VICTIMS

Introduction

The creation of an International Criminal Court provides a unique opportunity to give effect to the right of victims of atrocities to reparations.[262] Reparation to victims can take many forms, of which the establishment of the court and punishment of the perpetrators is one crucially important form. But there are other measures, from symbolic acts such as the erection of monuments recognizing that atrocities were committed, to direct acts of restitution or indemnification,[263] which play a crucial role in the reparation to individual victims or societies more broadly.[264] The making of reparations from perpetrator to victims can play a critical role in the healing process of victims and societies as a whole, and is itself a factor in preventing future violations. Reparation is an essential element in the administration of international justice.

---

[262] Provision in the ICC statute would not affect the international obligation of the state to provide reparations.

The right to reparations is enshrined in various international instruments. In some the principle is embodied in the right to an "effective remedy," as in Article 8 of the Universal Declaration of Human Rights and Article 2(3)(a) of the ICCPR, while others, such as the Convention against Torture and Other Cruel, Inhuman or Degrading Treatment or Punishment, contain express provision for an "enforceable right to fair and adequate compensation, including the means for as full rehabilitation as possible." (Article 14) The duty to "ensure" the rights protected in the American Convention on Human Rights has been interpreted by the Inter-American Court on Human Rights as involving the duty of the state to investigate, prosecute, punish, and provide adequate compensation. See *Velasquez Rodriguez* case, Series C, No.4, p.166. The duty of the state to make reparations to victims of serious violations of humanitarian law is made express in, for example, Article 3 of the Hague Convention IV, and the duty of a party to an international conflict to do so is contained in Article 91 of Additional Protocol I.

[263] It is particularly essential in the not infrequent circumstance in which the perpetrator of serious crimes has benefited financially from those wrongs, and the victims have suffered great economic hardship, that the Court be empowered to order restitution to the victims.

[264] See the "Basic Principles and Guidelines on the Right to Reparation for the Victims of [Gross] Violations of Human Rights and International Humanitarian Law," by the former special rapporteur of the Sub-Commission on Prevention of Discrimination and Protection of Minorities, Professor Theo van Boven pursuant to U.N. Commission on Human Rights resolution 1997/27, adopted on April 11, 1997. This document mentions symbolic reparations such as commemoration of victims or apology and public acknowledgment of the facts surrounding the crimes.

122

The ICC should have the power to make binding orders for reparation in favor of the victims of crimes within its jurisdiction. It is important that the Court be endowed both with appropriately strong powers to make binding and enforceable reparations orders, and the necessary flexibility to determine the most effective way of providing reparation in each concrete case. While orders will be made against the individuals responsible, upon a finding of guilt, it is extremely important that the statute clarify the obligation of state parties to comply with requests of the Court, to give effect to its judgments, and, where the perpetrator was a state actor, to satisfy the reparation orders.

Article 73[66]

• **Recommendation 1: The Court should have the power to award reparation to victims and their representatives. Delegates should strongly support retaining Article 73[66], with language empowering the Court, upon finding a defendant guilty, to make orders for reparations against the convicted person in favor of victims or their representatives.[265] Reparation should be defined broadly to include restitution, compensation, rehabilitation, satisfaction, and guarantees of non-repetition.**

Comment: The statute should reflect the rights of victims and their representatives to reparations under international law in respect of serious violations such as those falling within the jurisdiction of the Court. The most efficient way for the international community to realize this right would be through the mechanism of the ICC.[266]

Consistent with emerging international legal norms,[267] reparations must be understood, in a broad sense, to "include restitution, compensation,

---

[265] See also recommendations to Article 75[68](b) on including fines among the penalties to be added.

[266] The statute must recognize the reality that where national systems have, by definition, been unwilling or unable to administer criminal justice, it is unlikely that those systems will be able or willing to give effect to the victims' right to reparations.

[267] The Inter-American Court on Human Rights concluded, in its judgment on reparation in the *Velasquez Rodriguez* case, ibid, that "Reparation of harm brought about by the violation of an international obligation consists on full restitution which includes the restoration of the prior situation, the reparation of the consequences of the violation, and indemnification for patrimonial and non-patrimonial damages, including emotional harm."

rehabilitation, satisfaction and guarantees of non-repetition."[268]   The current text
of Article 73 should therefore be supported in so far as it deals with "reparation,"
rather than solely compensation, as in earlier incarnations of this Article. We
would encourage the inclusion of satisfaction and guarantees of non-repetition in
the list of permissible forms of reparation, to reflect the full breadth of types of
reparation recognized in the Basic Principles and Guidelines on the right to
Reparation for the Victims of [Gross] Violations of Human Rights and
International Humanitarian Law.[269]

The statute should adopt a broad approach to the definition of victim for these
purposes. For example, international bodies have recognized that society as a
whole can, in certain circumstances, be the victim of violations.
Correspondingly, the Court should be able to make such reparations orders as it
deems appropriate for the benefit of individuals or broader categories of
victims.[270]

The statute should establish the power of the Court to make such orders and the
Rules of Procedure should address practical questions such as the stage at which
victims would present their claims, what the form of such claims should be, and
the role of the Victim and Witness Protection Unit in facilitating such claims.

- *Recommendation:* **The statute should clarify that reparation orders
  against individuals, as judgments of the Courts, should be binding on
  state parties and directly enforced by them. In certain circumstances,
  state parties may also be obliged to satisfy reparation orders.**

Comment: While Article 73(66) establishes that reparation orders are to be
made binding against individual perpetrators, these orders constitute judgments
of the Court and, as such, states will be obliged by virtue of other provisions of
the statute[271] to enforce reparation orders. Accordingly, Article 73[66](5), which
currently provides that states parties "assist" victims in the enforcement of

---

[268] Theo van Boven, "Basic Principles and Guidelines on the Right to
Reparation..."
[269] Theo van Boven, "Basic Principles and Guidelines on the Right to
Reparation..."
[270] In these circumstances, given the vast numbers of individuals, their
representatives, and groups who may be victims of the crimes within the jurisdiction of the
Court, the power of the Court to award forms of reparation of a broader symbolic, rather than
purely financial, nature will be of particular importance.
[271] See Article 93[85] on enforcement of judgments.

orders, should be revised to reflect the mandatory nature of the obligation to enforce the Court's reparation orders.

Article 73[66] should be understood to be without prejudice to the duty of states to make reparations, as enshrined in international law. Moreover, in the case of defendants acting as state actors, the states should be bound to satisfy the reparation order on behalf of the individual perpetrators. In such cases, states should be given the opportunity to make relevant representations to the Court.[272]

- ***Recommendation :* Empower the Court, for the purpose of reparation, to order the seizure or forfeiture of assets that are either the objects of crime, or that are owned by or in the possession of the convicted person.**

Comment: If the above recommendation concerning reparations is to have practical effect, the Court should be empowered to provisionally forfeit and seize objects of crime or other assets belonging to the convicted person.[273] The Court should have the power to provisionally seize property during the investigation pending resolution of a claim for reparations. The Court must also be authorized to permanently retain any such assets in the event of a final judgment against the convicted person.

Article 79[72](a): Penalties

- ***Recommendation:* The proceeds of fines imposed by the court should benefit the victims of crime.**

Comment: This provision should be an addition, rather than alternative, to the above system for reparation. In itself this provision would be insufficient, as it would not necessarily involve any reparations between the perpetrator of a particular crime and the victim thereof. While this provision would not therefore provide for satisfaction of the victim's right to reparation as such, it would have a valuable complementary role, for example where judgements on damages cannot be enforced, or to compensate victims other than those with claims before

---

[272] If the individual was a state actor, then by virtue of general principles of vicarious responsibility the state may be bound to satisfy the reparation order on behalf of the individual perpetrator.

[273] This proposal was made at the August Preparatory Committee by the French delegation.

the ICC. We believe 79[72](a) to be the only appropriate proposal on allocation of fines.[274]

---

[274] In the section on penalties in the full report, we argue that fines should not be allocated to trial costs or to states.

SECTION L: PENALTIES

Introduction
In its quest to combat impunity, the ICC must ensure that the penalties it imposes reflect the egregious nature of the crimes within its jurisdiction. At the same time, in seeking to advance justice and the rule of law, it must ensure the unequivocal fairness of its sentences.

Structure of this section
The record of the August 1996 Preparatory Committee session on penalties noted that two groups of issues emerged from the negotiations on the question of penalties: "the types of penalties" and "the relevant laws." In Part 1 below we express the view that the penalties should be exhaustively set out in the statute. Specific recommendations in that section deal with which penalties we consider appropriate for application by the ICC, and which we consider inappropriate. In Part 2 we present some of the factors that the Court ought to take into consideration in determining the sentence in a particular case.

With regard to which laws should govern the application of penalties, as explained at Part 3 below, the ICC should rely on international and not national standards, and apply the penalties listed in the statute irrespective of the nationality of the convicted person.[275] The application of national laws could lead to sentences that are not commensurate with the gravity of the crimes in question, and it would be manifestly unjust for nationals of different states to receive unequal penalties in respect of the commission of the same crime.

Part 1. APPLICABLE PENALTIES

Part 7, Article 75

• **Recommendation 1: The statute should contain an exhaustive list of the types of penalties which the Court is empowered to impose. The language of Article 75 should clarify that only those penalties specified in the statute may be applied.**

---

[275] In this respect the provisions on penalties are but one manifestation of the important principle that the relevant laws and standards are international not national. See Section G of this report on applicable law and Section N on state cooperation and the prohibition on using national law as an excuse for noncompliance.

Comment: The principle of legality[276] demands that applicable penalties should be specified in the statute. As presently worded, the statute provides that the Court "may" impose one of a list of specified penalties, which may be construed to imply the discretion not to do so, but rather to decide to impose no penalty,[277] or to impose a different penalty not included in the list. This recommendation corresponds with the mandatory wording of the provision on penalties for the Statute of the International Criminal Tribunal for the Former Yugoslavia (ICTY).[278]

Article 75(a)

• **Recommendation: Imprisonment should be the principal penalty.**

Comment: Imprisonment is, in general, the most appropriate penalty for the crimes anticipated to come within the jurisdiction of the Court. Any system of imprisonment must, of course, respect the human rights of persons detained, including the need to have as an essential objective the "reform and social rehabilitation" of prisoners.[279] The standards which imprisonment ordered by the ICC would have to meet are set out in the Standard Minimum Rules for the Treatment of Prisoners[280] and the Body of Principles for the protection of All Persons under Any Form of Detention or Imprisonment.[281]

The statute should establish the appropriate penalties, while details concerning implementation should be addressed in the Rules.

---

[276] The principle of *nulla poena sine lege* demands that penalties be established in law. In this vein, Article 15 of the International Covenant on Civil and Public Rights (ICCPR), Article 7 of the European Convention for the Protection of Human Rights and Fundamental Freedoms, and Article 9 of the American Convention on Human Rights prohibit the imposition of a heavier penalty than the one that was applicable at the time when the criminal offence was committed.

[277] See recommendations on mitigation of punishment below.

[278] Article 24 of the statute of the ICTY provides that "the Trial Chamber shall be limited to imprisonment."

[279] See Article 10(3), the International Covenant on Civil and Political Rights.

[280] Economic and Social Council, Resolutions 663 C (XXIV) of July 31, 1957 and 2076 (LXII) of May 13, 1977.

[281] General Assembly resolution 43/173 of December 9, 1988.

- *Recommendation:* **Penalties should not be applicable to children as the ICC should have jurisdiction only over persons eighteen years old and older.**[282]

Comment: Children under the age of eighteen should not be tried by the International Criminal Court. As such, penalties should not be applicable to them and the bracketed text referring to persons under the age of eighteen should be deleted.

Article 75(b)

- *Recommendation:* **Include fines as an addition but not an alternative to imprisonment in respect of the core crimes, or for perjury or contempt of court.**

Comment: Given the gravity of the crimes within the Court's jurisdiction under Article 5[20], we consider the allocation of fines without custodial sentence inappropriate. The imposition of fines as an optional addition to custodial sentences should be supported. Fines could be imposed on their own, or with another penalty, in respect of perjury or contempt of court. Delegates should support retaining all bracketed text in Article 75(b).

Article 75(c)(I)

- *Recommendation 5:* **Empower the Court to prohibit the convicted person from holding an official or other position of responsibility.**

Comment: Persons found to have abused positions of responsibility should not be entitled to assume such positions in the future. It is an important deterrent to the future repetition of serious crimes that war criminals do not enjoy positions of control or authority within a state. Moreover, where persons have abused the expertise or the trust associated with their position, such as the doctors who carried out medical experimentation during the Second World War, the ICC should be empowered to disqualify such convicts from holding the position which they previously abused.

---

[282] See recommendations to Articles 6 to 9 on the jurisdiction of the Court and the minimum age of suspects/ accused persons.

Article 75 (c)(I) provides for disqualification from seeking public office for the period of imprisonment. While the principle of empowering the Court to disqualify convicts should be supported, it should be drawn more broadly, allowing the ICC to prohibit convicts from holding official or other positions wherever and for however long as the circumstances so demand.

Article 75(c)(ii) and (d)

• **Recommendation 6:** Include the power to order forfeiture of property.

Comment: The provision of Article 75(c)(ii) on forfeiture of property, and (d) on reparation, should be supported, as set out in the context of the recommendations on Article 73.

Article 75(e)

• **Recommendation 7:** Exclude the death penalty.

Comment: Human Rights Watch is opposed to the death penalty, irrespective of the crime or the process by virtue of which it is imposed, on account of its cruelty, and the inherent fallibility of any legal process. The imposition of capital punishment constitutes a violation of fundamental human rights.

Although capital punishment is not prohibited per se by international law, the inclusion of this penalty within the ICC statute would clearly be at odds with emerging international trends towards its abolition.[283] Any such inclusion would constitute an unacceptable regressive step in the development of international law in this field. It would further create a conflict with particular treaty obligations of states.[284]

---

[283] The Second Optional Protocol to the International Covenant on Civil and Political Rights aiming at the abolition of the death penalty, which entered into force 11 July 1991, prohibits the application of capital punishment for parties to the Protocol. This trend is also clear from the terms of the American Convention on Human Rights, which provides at Article 4(2) that the application of capital punishment "shall not be extended to crimes to which it does not presently apply," and at Article 4(3) that "the death penalty shall not be reestablished in States that have abolished it."

[284] Ibid.

The option in the current text[285] that the imposition of capital punishment should be permissible where there are aggravating circumstances,[286] should be opposed.

Part 2. DETERMINING THE SENTENCE IN THE PARTICULAR CASE

Article 77

- *Recommendation 1:* **The Court, in determining the sentence, shall take into account the gravity of the crime and the individual circumstances of the convicted person, among other factors.**

Comment: The Court should not be constrained by the rigidity of fixed penalties for certain categories of crimes. Rather, within the exhaustive list of permissible penalties, the Court should be able to evaluate which penalties are appropriate and how they should be applied in particular cases. The obligation of the Court to evaluate the gravity of the offense[287] and all relevant circumstances is important to ensure that justice can be done in any particular case.

- *Recommendation 2:* **The statute should include an illustrative, non-exhaustive list of mitigating and aggravating factors.**

Comment: Linked to the essential flexibility of the Court in determining the appropriate penalty in the particular circumstances is the power of the Court to consider mitigating and/or aggravating factors. Article 77(1) currently states that in determining the sentence, the Court shall take into account "the individual circumstances of the convicted person," but does not list any of the possible mitigating and aggravating circumstances.

Including an illustrative list gives the Court guidance as to the sort of factors that it should consider relevant for this purpose, while not inhibiting its ability to respond to the very different and perhaps unforeseen circumstances which may arise in a particular case.

---

[285] This text was presented as a joint proposal by a group of states, namely Algeria, Libya, Egypt, Jordan, and Kuwait.

[286] The proponents argue that not to do so would disregard practice in many countries. In this regard, see the arguments concerning applicable law, above.

[287] In Section A we oppose the proposal that only war crimes committed on a massive scale, or pursuant to a plan or policy, should come within the jurisdiction of the Court. However, the scale on which the crime was committed is relevant to the gravity of the crime and is an example of the sort of factor to be taken into account in sentencing.

The inclusion of a mitigating factor in the list should not, of course, oblige the Court to alter the punishment it would otherwise impose but for the existence of the factor. Rather, it gives the Court the flexibility to consider whether the presence of the factor does, in the totality of the circumstances, justify a lesser punishment.

- *Recommendation 3:* Include the following mitigating factors in the non-exhaustive list:
- the age of the convicted person at the time of committing the crime and other relevant stages, such as the time of recruitment into armed forces, together with the nature of any such recruitment;[288]
- diminished mental capacity;
- superior orders, and resistance the convicted person showed to the commission of the crime;
- duress, coercion, or other form of pressure to which the convicted person was subject;
- lack of dangerousness and ability of the convicted person to be reformed.

Comment: In many cases, the circumstances enumerated above do not exonerate responsibility and should not therefore constitute one of the established defenses applicable by the ICC.[289] The Court should, however, be endowed with the necessary flexibility to take into account a broad range of factors in determining the appropriate sentence in any particular case. The Court should consider, on a case by case basis, whether these factors justify the imposition of a lesser punishment than would otherwise be appropriate.

The statutes of the International Criminal Tribunals for the Former Yugoslavia and Rwanda allow for superior orders, for example, to be taken into account as a mitigating factor.[290] This, and the resistance the convicted person showed to the commission of the crime should be an important factor for the Court to take into account, as should the degree of duress or coercion to which the guilty person

---

[288] See the recommendation in the Section B concerning the minimum age of persons over whom the Court should have jurisdiction.

[289] See Section F on defenses.

[290] Art. 6(4) of the statute for the International Criminal Tribunal for Rwanda states that "the fact that an accused person acted pursuant to an order of a Government or of a superior shall not relieve him or her of criminal responsibility, but may be considered in mitigation of punishment if the International Criminal Tribunal for Rwanda determines that justice so requires."

was subject. The Appeals Chamber of the International Criminal Tribunal for the Former Yugoslavia in the case of Prosecutor v. Erdomovic also recognized "extreme necessity arising from duress and coercion" as a mitigating factor.[291] The Trial Chamber's decision in the Erdomovic case endorsed the appropriateness of considering the present lack of dangerousness and ability of the convicted person to be reformed as mitigating factors.

With regard specifically to the age of the accused, Human Rights Watch believes that eighteen must be the relevant age for the purposes of allowing the ICC to exercise jurisdiction, and therefore the question of mitigation of punishment for offenders under eighteen at the time of commission of the offense does not arise.[292] However, even with regard to offenders over the age of eighteen, the youth of the offender should be taken into account, as should the age at which he or she was recruited into the armed force, particularly where that recruitment or participation was compelled, or where he or she was forced at a young age to commit crimes of the sort in question. Taking into account the age of the convicted person is consistent with the approach adopted by the Appeals Chamber of the International Criminal Tribunal for the Former Yugoslavia.[293]

Any list should, however, omit cultural, traditional, or religious beliefs adhered to by individuals as mitigating or extenuating circumstances in the commission of egregious human rights violations. Discrimination and cultural prejudice may indeed be the motivating element behind these crimes, and it is precisely such discrimination and its effects that are universally condemned in international human rights instruments and humanitarian law.[294]

---

[291] Prosecutor v. Erdomovic, ICTY, IT-96-22-A, (7 October 1997).

[292] See Part 3 below.

[293] See the Erdomovic case, ibid.

[294] National courts frequently take into consideration in sentencing or determining criminal liability the cultural tradition of an accused, especially where that tradition condones violence against women. Mitigation of sentence or culpability is common, for example, in "honor" killings, where a husband murders his allegedly adulterous wife, as in Egypt and other countries. In the United States, the justice system has mitigated sentences for Asian immigrants convicted of crimes of violence against women on the basis of their cultural backgrounds.

Part 3. APPLICABLE NATIONAL LEGAL STANDARDS

Article 78

- *Recommendation:* **There should be a uniform, not variable, standard for penalties.**[295] **As such Article 78 Option 2 should be retained and Option 1, which states that, in determining sentence, the Court may or shall take into account penalties provided for in specified national laws should be deleted.**

Comment: As stated in the introduction, to ensure the equitable and universal application of penalties, the ICC must make its sentencing decisions independently of national laws. Allowing the Court to consider national penalties would, in view of the vast differences in standards between jurisdictions, lead to undesirable uncertainty in this important aspect of the rights of accused or convicted persons.

Furthermore, the fact that many legal systems impose discriminatory or trivial penalties for certain types of crimes militates against giving the ICC discretion to defer to national penalties in sentencing. Discriminatory national penalties are indicated, for instance, by the fact that, in certain jurisdictions, male perpetrators of violent crimes against women can allege mitigating factors -- as in "heat of passion" crimes -- that are denied to women accused of identical crimes against men. An example of the application of trivial national penalties would be the strikingly low penalties for rape in certain countries as a result of the crime of rape being defined as a crime of moral turpitude or a violation of a woman's honor, rather than an as act of violence to the person. Finally, the injustice in the differential treatment of two persons convicted of the same crime on the sole basis of nationality, for example, is inconsistent with the universality of the Court.

Article 79

- *Recommendation 2:* **The fines collected by the Court and the assets forfeited in accordance with Article 75 should be applied toward the reparation of victims, and not allocated to any state nor toward defraying the cost of the trial.**

---

[295] See also comments under recommendation to Article 20[14] on Applicable Law.

Comment: The current text proposes that fines may be transferred to the state whose nationals were the victims of the crimes or to defraying the cost of the trial. Given the common involvement of states directly or indirectly in the commission of the crimes anticipated to come within the jurisdiction of the Court, the first provision should be opposed.[296] While the objective of this provision--to ensure that victims of crime be compensated--should be supported, Article 79(a) envisages creation of a trust fund administered by an objective entity would be a preferable mechanism to achieve this end. With regard to the proposal that fines might go towards funding the administration of the Court, this may bring into question the impartiality of the Court. The statute should not render the Court vulnerable to allegations as to conflict of interest in the determination of appropriate penalties or the amount of a particular fine.

---

[296]As noted in Section K, if the convict was a state actor, the state may in fact be vicariously liable, not for fines imposed, but for orders of reparation. It would be absurd for a state to be liable to pay compensation under one order of the Court, and then entitled to request receipt of the sums recovered from fines imposed against its agents by virtue of another. It would, of course, be open to the Court in such circumstances to refuse to pay the proceeds to the state, but this scenario exposes the tension in involving the State as a potential recipient of the proceeds of fines.

SECTION M: THE PROTECTION OF NATIONAL SECURITY

Structure of this Section

This section supports the proposal that national security concerns should be dealt with in a freestanding article, which should then be applied to all relevant provisions of the statute. After introductory comments, we make recommendations on the content of that freestanding article, including specific comments on the provisions in Option 2 of Article 71[64].[297] Recommendations then follow concerning the specific articles which have dealt with national security and related questions of confidentiality. Specific concerns of relevance to each article are pointed out, although in general, a strong freestanding article containing the relevant principles will address these specific concerns.

The protection of legitimate interests

States have legitimate security interests which, in the course of cooperating with the ICC, they will seek to protect. It would be unrealistic and indeed irresponsible for an international court to be blind to interests such as the protection of national security. As such, it should be understood that the ICC will operate with due judicial regard for such interests, and due deference to the state's assessment of when they may be in jeopardy. Given the mandate of the International Criminal Court, however, these interests must be balanced against other important and potentially competing interests. These would include the interests of victims, and of the international community as a whole in seeing an end to impunity in respect of the "most serious crimes of concern to the international community...."[298] Deference to *national* security must be tempered by the need to ensure the protection of *international* security, which is seriously compromised by the commission of heinous crimes and the impunity that so often surrounds them.

There are also compelling interests of the accused and of the international community in ensuring that judgments of the Court are just, rendered in the light of all relevant information, and that the right to a fair trial is absolutely guaranteed. To meet the challenge of effectively administering international

---

[297] See Option 2 in Article 71[64], submitted as Article X by the delegation of the United Kingdom of Great Britain and Northern Ireland, at the March/April 1998 Preparatory Committee on the establishment of an ICC, A/AC.249/1998/WG.4/DP20

[298] Preamble to the draft statute.

justice, the Court will be reliant on the provision of information by states. Through intelligence and other sources, states will often have access to information concerning the commission of crimes within the Court's jurisdiction that will be essential to ensuring that perpetrators of these serious crimes can be brought to justice. If exculpatory or probative information is withheld by states, miscarriages of justice may ensue. We believe that it is critical to the credibility of the ICC that it observe unequivocally the right of the accused to prepare his or her defense, an essential component of which is access to information of potential relevance to the defense.

The scope of the national security privilege

Given the fundamental nature of these interests, any national security privilege which might impinge upon them must be strictly formulated. The term "national security," is in our view preferable to broader, vague or potentially wide-ranging formulations such as *ordre public* or "other essential interests," contained in one draft article.

Moreover, and of critical importance, is that it must ultimately be for the Court to determine the applicability of the exception in any concrete case. Delegates should follow the guidance of the Trial Chamber of the International Criminal Tribunal for the Former Yugoslavia in the case of the *Prosecutor v. Tihomir Blaskic*, which stated: "taking into account the interests at stake, namely those of the international community in the restoration of peace and the bringing of justice to the former Yugoslavia, the international tribunal is best positioned to ascertain the legitimacy of a claim of privilege."[299]

The Court's statute must ensure that the national security exception applies only in cases where there is a legitimate concern justifying the measures sought and cannot be relied upon by states (or by individuals supported by states)[300] as a pretext for interfering with the course of justice. Any provision for a national security exception must not facilitate the withholding of information to avoid incriminating the state's political leadership, or to shield possible criminals from prosecution.

---

[299] IT 95-14PT, July 18, 1997 p.149.
[300] As provided for in Article 71[64], which allows an individual to assert national security and the state to verify the claim.

The statute should clearly establish the relevant criteria for assessing genuine and serious prejudice to national security, and the role of the Court as the ultimate arbiter of the issue.

FREESTANDING ARTICLE ON THE PROTECTION OF NATIONAL SECURITY INTERESTS

Article 71[64]

- *Recommendation 1: the framework*
The inclusion in the statute of a freestanding provision relating to the protection of national security interests should be supported.

Comment: The initiative to create a freestanding provision reflects the fact that national security concerns arise in relation to a number of distinct provision in different parts of the statute. The principles underlying the treatment of these various provisions ought to be the same, although there are additional concerns specific to particular articles.[301] The existence of one article dedicated to enshrining these common principles would provide greater clarity and ensure consistency in the treatment of this important issue throughout the statute. The framework provided by Option 2 of Article 71 should therefore be supported.[302] It should be applicable to Articles 58[51](10) and 68(9)[61],[303] and 90[82](2)[304] of the statute and, where appropriate, Article 90(6)[82(5)][305].

- *Recommendation 2: The principles*
Where a state declares that its national security would be seriously prejudiced by the application of the general rules regarding evidence and the duty to cooperate, the Court should be empowered to grant exceptions to these general rules. The freestanding article should provide for cooperative measures to be taken to resolve conflicts regarding the treatment of sensitive information and avoid the need for adjudication of the matter. Where the matter cannot be resolved, a mechanism should be

---

[301] Specific comments of relevance to the particular provisions are set out below.

[302] As stated in Section E on complementarity, this provision may apply not only to those articles indicated at paragraph 1, but also to Article 90[82](5).

[303] This article relates to the protection of victims and witnesses.

[304] This article relates to the possible grounds for refusing other forms of cooperation.

[305] This article relates to information provided for the purposes of generating evidence.

established to ensure that states have adequate opportunity to make confidential representations to the Court as to the serious prejudice to their national security which would result from compliance with the request. Finally, the statute must make clear that ultimate authority rests with the ICC, and not the state concerned, to determine whether an exception shall be granted on the basis of national security in the particular cases.

Comment: A state's interest in protecting its national security, within the meaning attributed to the term contained in widely ratified human rights instruments,[306] is entirely legitimate. More wide-ranging formulations contained in the current draft statute[307] create uncertainty and susceptibility to abuse and should be deleted.[308]

It is critical that the statute protect the ultimate authority of the Court to determine any claim made on the basis of national security. A mechanism should be established whereby states can lodge claims and have a full opportunity to explain the national security concerns to the Court, with the confidentiality of those proceedings safeguarded. In the exceptional circumstances where national security is invoked, this may involve in camera or *ex parte* hearings.[309] While we believe the precise details as to the nature of

---

[306] National security is referred to in Articles 12, 13, 14, 19, 21 and 22 of the International Covenant on Civil and Political Rights (ICCPR), as a justification for restricting certain rights protected in that instrument. One commentary on the provisions states that "'National' indicates that the anticipated danger must relate to the country as a whole...." while security relates to the "use of force or threat of force against the political independence or territorial integrity of another state." Lockwood, Finn and Jubinsky, "Working Paper for the Committee of Experts on Limitation Provisions," *Human Rights Quarterly*, vol. 7, no.1 (February 1985), p.71.

[307] See Article 90[82](2) which refers to *"ordre public* as other essential interests."

[308] The importance of narrowing the scope of national security exceptions and the dangers associated with not doing so was expressed by the drafters of the International Covenant on Civil and Political Rights (ICCPR), in the following terms: "If limitations were not clearly defined, but couched in general terms, there was little guarantee that rights would not be violated....In the name of 'public order' many a saintly character has been crucified, in the name of 'national security' many a patriot guillotined." 10 UN GAOR Annexes (Agenda item 28) p.9, UN Doc, A/2929 (1955).

[309] Guidance should be sought from the judgment of the Trial Chamber of the ICTY in the aforementioned *Prosecutor v. Tihomir Blaskic* case which stated, at para.148: "Consequently, for the purpose of determining the validity of the assertions of a particular state relating to national security concerns, the Trial Chamber may hold in camera hearings,

such mechanisms could be elaborated in the rules of the Court,[310] we support the measures set out in paragraph 4 of Option 2 of Article 71[64]. It should be necessary to utilize such measures only exceptionally, and the statute should provide for all efforts to be taken by both the Court and the state concerned to resolve disputes by cooperative means.

Option 2 of Article 71 [Article X]

- *Recommendation*: **Paragraphs (1) to (4) of Option 2 of Article 71 should be supported as reflective of the principles set out in the preceding recommendation. Most critically, the provision authorizes the ICC to make the final determination regarding any claim based on national security. The option should, however, be amended, to establish a more feasible standard for the assessment of whether a claim is founded or unfounded.**

Option 2 of Article 71 represents a major step forward in negotiations on this difficult issue. One of the essential features of this proposal is that it endows the Court with the ultimate authority, in certain circumstances, to make the determination as to the claim of national security. In this key respect, it is far preferable to the alternative proposals on the table at this stage[311] that would enable national security to be used as an absolute bar to the Court's ability to control its own proceedings. Option 2 of Article 71[64] also contains helpful provisions concerning cooperation between states and the ICC, and proposes mechanisms, such as *in camera* hearings, that provide appropriate safeguards to ensure the protection of legitimate national security interests.

While Option 2 of Article 71[64], paragraphs (1) to (4), should therefore be supported, the wording of paragraph (5) should be amended. The circumstances in which the Court will disregard a state's own assessment of the threat to its

---

in a manner consistent with rules 66© and Rule 79. Furthermore, with a view to safeguard the secrecy of the information it may initially conduct ex parte hearings in a manner analogous to that provided to the Trial Chamber or Judge and not necessarily to the requesting party...."

[310] Proposals regarding the Regulations of the Court are contained at Article 53. A proposal that detailed provisions regarding national security be dealt with in the regulations was made in the context of former Article 33[27] and appears in the current draft text of that Article, current Article 58[51](5)(f).

[311] See the proposals submitted to the March/April Preparatory Committee by the delegations of the United States of America and France.

national security will be exceptional, and the text as it stands is an attempt to reflect this. However, the exceptional circumstances set out in paragraph (5) may impose an impossibly onerous burden on the Court and constitute an insurmountable impediment to its ability to function. Under the present text of this article, the Court would have to be satisfied that each of the circumstances referred to in paragraph (5) exists; that is, for example that it is "clear from the State's action that it is not acting in good faith towards the Court...," and that "the Court is satisfied that the claim[312] is manifestly without foundation."

Bad faith should not be part of the relevant criteria. In the absence of bad faith, a state may make an entirely unfounded claim, for example, due to a misunderstanding as to the meaning or scope of the national security privilege under the statute. In this circumstance the Court should retain authority over the interpretation and application of the statute. Or alternatively, the Court may well not, in practice, have access to sufficient information on the basis of which to demonstrate clear bad faith. In either case, it should be sufficient that the Court, after exhausting all of the steps embodied in Option 2 of Article 71[64] and listening to all arguments the relevant state may wish to pose, determine that a national security claim is unfounded, without having to prove bad faith. The ICC must make those determinations necessary for the proper conduct of proceedings before it; it should not have to engage in the factually difficult and politically sensitive task of judging the bona fides or mala fides of individual states.

STATE COOPERATION: CHALLENGING A REQUEST FROM THE COURT

Article 90[82](2) Option 2(d)

- **Recommendation 1:** The statute should not allow states, under any circumstances, to "deny" a request for cooperation. The Court and not the state is the ultimate arbiter of state parties obligations toward the Court. Reference should be made to the freestanding article, as embodying the relevant criterion and mechanisms for challenging a request, on the basis of the harm to a state's national security that would ensue. Serious prejudice to national security should therefore be the criterion for invoking the provisions of this article, and references

---

[312] The "claim" is a claim by a state that its interests would be prejudiced by disclosure.

to "*ordre public*" or the undefined and potentially wide-reaching term "essential interests" should be deleted. The reference to evidence being withheld from the Court on the basis that it "relates to" national security or defense, where there was in fact no prejudice to national security interests, should be deleted.

Comment: Both Article 90[82](2) and Option 3 of Article 71[64][313] make reference to "denying a request" for cooperation on specified national security grounds and, as set out in the preceding section of this commentary, should be deleted. A state would not be legally entitled to "refuse," but rather would be able to petition that the Court, in the light of its submissions, withdraw or alter a request.[314] The inappropriateness of broader terms than national security has already been commented upon. Only in the context of Article 90[82](2) does the criteria of "*ordre public*" and "other essential interests" appear in the statute, and delegates are urged to delete these unclear and potentially sweeping terms.

The reference to evidence which "relates to" national security or defense is similarly appropriate. Any national security or other provision which may affect the fundamental obligations and interests of the international community and to a defendant in seeing justice done should only be permissible where there is a well-founded basis for believing that compliance with the request would seriously prejudice national security. Potentially, a great deal of material could relate in some tangential sense to national security, without being harmful to it; this provision could lead to potentially relevant material being withheld from the Court, and therefore a defendant.

Reference to the standard in a freestanding article, such as Option 2 of Article 71[64], rather than the imposition of different criterion for each article, would avoid these problems.

---

[313] This is a slightly more restrictive alternative to Article 90[82](2), presented by the delegation of the United States during the sixth Preparatory Committee session

[314] We recognize that this heading applies to other "grounds" beyond national security. As Human Rights Watch opposes the inclusion of unilateral "grounds of refusal," and supports the ultimate authority of the Court to determine such matters, this deletion would be consistent with our views on the question of state cooperation and compliance.

CRIMINAL PROCEDURE: MEASURES TO PROTECT SENSITIVE
INFORMATION

Article 68(9)[61]

- *Recommendation:* **The ability of states to seek measures of protection from the Court to protect the life or physical integrity of their agents and servants should be supported. The protection of sensitive information, which unlike the protection of life and safety can properly be regarded as a national security issue as such, should be subject to the terms of the freestanding article.**

Comment: The disclosure of information may, in certain circumstances, expose agents of the state to physical danger and the Court should be empowered to take measures it deems appropriate to address those concerns, consistent with the rights of the accused. This may include measures relating to the manner in which evidence is presented, such as in camera hearings, the use of pseudonyms, voice-altering mechanisms, or redaction of documents, in line with paragraph (4) of Option 2 of Article 71[64].

Sensitive information, the disclosure of which would seriously prejudice national security, could be protected within the framework of the freestanding national security article.

CRIMINAL PROCEDURE: DISCLOSURE

Article 58(10)(f)[51]

- *Recommendation*: **The freestanding article would apply to this provision for the Court to make orders for the non-disclosure or protection of documents or information provided by a state on the grounds the disclosure would endanger or prejudice national security. The article should therefore provide that only serious prejudice to national security would justify an order for non-disclosure. Broader formulations, such as endangering "national defense," in the absence of any real harm should be excluded.[315] A mechanism for representations to be made by the state, in accordance with previous recommendations, should also be established.**

---

[315] See definition set out in the context of Article 90[82](2)above.

Comment: The prosecutor has a *duty* to disclose to the defense all evidence of potential relevance. As an exception to this, non-disclosure of information relevant to the defense must be exceptional. We support endowing the Pre-Trial Chamber with the power to review disclosure and determine the applicability or otherwise of any national security privilege, as established in the freestanding article.

CRIMINAL PROCEDURE: WITNESS INVOCATION OF NATIONAL SECURITY

Article 71[64]

- *Recommendation:* The provision allowing individuals to "invoke restrictions provided for in his national law and designed to prevent the disclosure of confidential information connected with national security and national defense" should be amended. The objective criteria established in the freestanding article for the assessment of any claim to national security should also apply to this article. This would ensure that the statute, and not variable national laws, would provide the benchmark to determine the Court's access to information or the use to which information can be put by the Court in the exercise of its functions. The statute should, however, provide that states will not prosecute individuals solely for giving evidence to the Court in violation of national law.

Comment: As set out above, any national security privilege must be established according to objective criteria and be clearly defined. It is for the Court to interpret and apply that definition, determining whether the national security privilege justifies non-disclosure in any given case. Variable national law should not determine the Court's access to information or the use to which information can be put by the Court in the exercise of its functions.

Witnesses will, however, have a legitimate concern to avoid falling afoul of national criminal laws through giving evidence to the ICC; the Court should not force an individual to incur punishment as a result of violating his or her national criminal law. Where the Court rejects a national security claim in these circumstances, the State should not then prosecute the individual for giving evidence to the Court in violation of national law. This would clearly be unfair to the witness in question and would additionally impede the Court's ability to secure important evidence. If the terms of national laws conflict with a state's obligations under the statute, as interpreted by the Court, the state must take necessary steps to give legal effect to its international obligations.[316]

---

[316] The Vienna Convention on the Law of International Treaties, adopted May 23, 1969, sets out the principle of *pacta sunt servanda* in Article 26, and Article 27 establishes the related principle that, in the event of a conflict between national and international law, the latter prevails: "Internal law and observance of treaties: A party may not invoke the provision of its internal law as justification for its failure to perform a treaty...."

SECTION N: INTERNATIONAL COOPERATION AND JUDICIAL ASSISTANCE

Introduction

The full and timely cooperation of states at every stage of the criminal process is critical to the success and integrity of the International Criminal Court. The Court, like any national court, must be able to compel the production of evidence, mandate that suspects be arrested and brought before it, and enforce judgments; yet it will be reliant on states to carry out these functions. Even if in all other respects the Court were to have full powers, its effectiveness in vindicating justice for the worst violations of human rights would be vitiated should its statute give license for states to deny compliance with its requests.

The experience of the *ad hoc* tribunals for Former Yugoslavia and Rwanda demonstrates the importance of the Court having full powers in the area of state cooperation to ensure that the Court's operation and existence are not rendered meaningless. The statutes, powers and practices of the *ad hoc* tribunals must be taken as the minimum baseline for framing cooperation duties with respect to the permanent Court. To the extent that the draft statute falls below that bare minimum, it must be strengthened so that the Court will not represent a step backward in the fight against impunity.

To ensure that the Court is capable of operating both effectively and independently, according to the highest standards of justice, the provisions of Part 9 must be framed by the following principles.

Cooperation must be defined as a matter of legal obligation that the Court may rely upon, rather than as an uncertain variable, subject to the will or circumstances of any particular state. The duty to fulfill the Court's requests should be clearly established by the treaty and freely assumed by state parties upon ratification or accession. To this end, Human Rights Watch believes it is essential that the formulation of this duty be in terms of compliance with Court requests, rather than in terms of "cooperation," which as a generic term may allow state parties to fall short of full compliance.

Moreover, the duty of the requested state to comply must entail timely action. Delay is capable of defeating justice, particularly in the context of criminal prosecutions where evidence, testimonial or other, may be destroyed, lost or its value diminished over time. Provisional measures must be taken by the state pending the Court's adjudication of disputes over cooperation matters.

146

Of key importance is the principle of the primacy of international obligations over national law. Without shared recognition of this principle, numerous barriers would stand in the way of the Court's proper functions, even for states with every intention to be fully cooperative. National laws and rules, for example, should not be used to restrict the Court in questioning any and all witnesses privately, in accessing restricted areas for investigation, or in securing material evidence or assets necessary to enforce judgments. Nor should national laws be the yardstick for assessing the legality of the Court's requests; challenges should be referred to the Court itself for adjudication in light of the Court's own statute and international law. State claims that considerations such as national security prevail over full compliance must be subject to the Court's review and not allowed to constitute a unilaterally imposed escape clause.

To ensure that this fundamental principle is the bedrock for relations between the Court and state parties, the preamble of the draft statute should explicitly set out that state parties may not invoke domestic law as a justification for failing to give full effect to this treaty. This principle is a rule of customary international law.[317] Although customary international law requires that state parties amend internal laws to comply with international law, the Court's statute should explicitly set forth the requirement of amending such laws that may obstruct cooperation, and promptly frame implementing legislation where necessary. Both the statute and its negotiating record should make clear that state parties shall not unilaterally decide the legitimacy of cooperation requests, but rather will ensure that such issues are referred to the Court and that the decisions of the Court are given the full force of law by national courts.

The Court's effectiveness might be similarly undercut were state parties to rely on other international agreements to avoid surrendering suspects to the Court or cooperating with its investigations pending resolution of the conflict of laws. It is a fundamental principle of international law that state parties may not normally amend their obligations flowing from multilateral treaties by concluding

---

[317] This reflects Article 27 of the United Nations Convention on the Law of Treaties, signed at Vienna on May 23, 1969, entered into force on January 27, 1980, which states that: "A party may not invoke the provisions of its internal law as justification for its failure to perform a treaty." It is well established that Article 27 embodies a "long accepted rule of customary law." (Louis Henkin, Richard Crawford Pugh, Oscar Schachter, Hans Smit, *International Law: Cases and Materials*, West Publishing, St. Paul, MN, Second Edition, 1987; p. 434). Advisory Opinion on Treatment of Polish Nationals in Danzig, 1932 P.C.I.J., Ser. A/B, No. 44, at 22.

subsequent bilateral treaties. The Court's statute should deny legal effect to subsequent agreements that modify the obligations between two or more state parties under the treaty, such as subsequent bilateral extradition arrangements.

Finally, although many of the procedures outlined in this section of the draft statute have roots in the practice of extradition and mutual assistance, neither extradition nor mutual assistance agreements are an appropriate paradigm for cooperation with an international body, as opposed to cooperation between two sovereign states. The premise of the International Criminal Court is that it will administer justice according to the highest international, rather than national, standards, in cases of the most grave international crimes which carry universal jurisdiction. Traditional exceptions and allowances for refusal of cooperation in the context of extradition or mutual assistance, such as the concept of political offenses, nationality of the suspect, or procedural fairness concerns, should be inapplicable given the international nature of the Court, the strict and well-defined terms of its statutory jurisdiction, and its governance under international standards of justice.

THE OBLIGATION TO COMPLY

Article 85[77]: Cooperation and judicial assistance

- **Recommendation: Define the nature of the obligation as one of full compliance without undue delay. Amend Article 85[77](1) in line with Article 29 of the statute of the International Criminal Tribunal for Former Yugoslavia and Article 28 of the statute of the International Criminal Tribunal for Rwanda. As such, the statute should provide that state parties shall <u>fully comply without undue delay</u> with any request for assistance or order issued by the Court in connection with criminal investigations and proceedings under this statute.**

Comment: As currently written, the draft provision calls into question whether the Court will even have the powers of the current *ad hoc* tribunals to ensure compliance with its requests and decisions. The statute must leave no doubt as to the nature of a state parties obligation to comply with the Court's requests, precisely because such compliance is essential for it to function at all. Human Rights Watch strongly urges the use of the term "comply" rather than "cooperate," because the latter term may imply that actions short of full compliance are sufficient. Compliance must be understood as prompt action, taking into account the time limits pertinent to any given case. Finally, compliance must be "full" in nature, requiring the state to make reasonable use of all resources and means at its disposal in carrying out the request.

In our view, this provision is pivotal to the success of resolving disputes concerning cooperation request in a manner that does not frustrate the basic functioning of the Court. The vague duty of "cooperation" is open to the interpretation that a state must act in good faith but may not be 'able' to satisfy the request, for example due to inconsistent national laws. The duty of compliance underscores the obligation on states to ensure that the request is satisfied, including giving the international treaty priority over domestic laws and regulations.

Moreover, in the interests of consistency, this general provision should be consistent with other provisions of the statute, and reflect the language of the sections dealing with the transfer of persons to the Court[318] and other forms of cooperation,[319] both of which express the obligation as one of compliance with requests.

DELETION OF GROUNDS FOR REFUSAL

Article 87[79] and 90[82](2): Grounds for refusal and denial of requests

- **Recommendation: Consistent with the duty to comply, it should not be within the unilateral power of state parties to refuse requests from the Court, relating either to the transfer of persons or any other matter. The references to "grounds for refusal" and "a state party may deny a request..." in Articles 87[79](2) and 90[82](2) should therefore be deleted. If compliance would prejudice national security interests,[320] a provision should be made in the statute for the state to petition the Court to set aside the request, under the terms of the proposed free-standing article on national security.[321] As it would ultimately be for the Court, in accordance with mechanisms set out in the freestanding article, to make the determination on the applicability or otherwise of the national security exception, this should not constitute grounds for refusal but rather for petition or challenge.**

Comment: States are under an obligation to cooperate with the Court and must be clearly obliged to comply with its requests, as set out above. Such obligation

---

[318] Article 87[79].

[319] Article 90[82].

[320] This would only arise in the context of Article 90[82](2); an exception to the duty to transfer could not be justified by national security, while an exception related to the protection of information may be.

[321] See recommendations in Section M.

will be rendered meaningless of the state is able to "refuse" to comply in particular circumstances. Provisions apparently allowing states unilaterally to "refuse" or "deny" requests could paralyze the Court.

Human Rights Watch recognizes that there are exceptional circumstances where a state party should not be obliged to cooperate under the statute, namely where compliance would constitute a threat to a state's national security interests. The statute should make provision for the state to petition the Court to set aside the request on that basis. Similarly, Article 87[79](3) provides for an "[a]pplication to the Court to set [requests] aside...." This article could be used as an acceptable framework for an alternative to the grounds for refusal provisions currently in the text.[322] Following state petition, the Court should uphold the challenge where it finds the claim to be well founded, in accordance with the statute.

The current draft of Article 87[79] refers to states refusing to comply with a request on the basis that a case is inadmissible under Article 15[11]. It is, of course, for the Court to determine the admissibility of a case. This would be entirely inconsistent with, and undermine, other provisions of the statute. It would be disastrous for this cooperation provision to enable states to usurp the judicial function of the Court to determinations as to complementarity and admissibility.

EXCLUDING NATIONAL LAWS AS A BASIS FOR NON COMPLIANCE

Article 87[79]: national law governing transfer of an accused to the Court

• **Recommendation: Article 87[79](2), which provides for the national law of a requested state to govern the conditions for complying with or denying a request for transfer, should be amended to clarify that national laws can never constitute an excuse for not complying with a request from the Court.**

---

[322] Article 87[79](3), provides for "[a]pplication to the Court to set aside [surrender][transfer][extradition]." Clearly, the use of extradition terminology is, as explained in the introduction, inappropriate, given the very different nature of relations between state parties and the ICC and the relation between two equal sovereign states. The suggestion is that the principle of applying to set aside a request enshrined at this part of the statute may, however, prove useful. With regard to the terms of Article 87[79](3) concerning the states right to delay compliance pending resolution of the dispute before the Court, see comment below on the adoption of provisional measures.

Comment: The obligation of the requested state to comply with the Court on this fundamental issue of transfer of the accused is an essential element of the statute, without which prosecution of serious criminals will not be possible. The statute must not, therefore, allow a state to avoid compliance with this obligation on the basis of its internal law. Rather, the fundamental principle of the supremacy of international law, and the duty of a state to change its internal law so far as necessary to accommodate its international obligations, applies.

Moreover, national laws vary greatly, creating vastly differential standards in the treatment of different cases. Such variable national laws should not control or limit the Court's ability to discharge its essential functions. Rather, the nature of a state's obligations should be governed by the statute and principles of international law.

Article 87(7): Proceedings in a requested state

- *Recommendation:* **Delete Article 87(7), which contains provision regarding the right of provides for the person whose transfer is sought to challenge that transfer in domestic courts.**

Comment: In line with the previous recommendation, the ICC should be governed by international law and general principles, not national laws and proceedings. Provisions regarding procedures that may exist on the national level have no place in the statute. The provision implies that national laws or the outcome of proceedings before domestic courts could constitute a legitimate reason for not complying with requests from the Court. Rather, as explained above, national laws must be brought into line with international obligations in the event of a divergence, and can never justify non-compliance by state parties. The provision should therefore be deleted.

THE POWER TO ORDER PROVISIONAL MEASURES

Article 87[79] and 90[82](2): No reference to provisional measures

- *Recommendation:* **The Court should have the power to request that a state take provisional measures, in particular pending the resolution of a petition to set aside a request from the Court. In addition to the power to order provisional arrest,[323] the statute should empower the Court to**

---

[323] Article 89[81].

request other measures the Court may deem necessary for the effective discharge of its mandate.

Comment: Human Rights Watch is very concerned that the current draft does not contain an article relating to the Court's power to order provisional measures, pending a resolution of any dispute relating to cooperation. The provision which appeared in earlier drafts of the statute has been omitted from the latest text.[324] Rather, the current draft of Article 87[79](3) simply provides that a state may 'delay' complying with a request pending a determination of disputes relating to requests, without specific reference to the need for provisional measures. In certain circumstances, delay may prove catastrophic to the future possibility of bringing an individual to justice. Provisional arrest is clearly a key measure, and one which is explicitly addressed in the latest text. However, other measures short of provisional arrest, such as the provisional seizure of assets, measures for the protection of victims and witnesses and preservation of evidence, may likewise prove essential to ensure that justice can be done.

PRIORITY OF REQUESTS OF THE COURT OVER OTHER STATE PARTIES

Article 87[79](4): Parallel requests from the Court and states

- **Recommendation: The text should clarify that states parties should always give priority to Court requests over requests from other state parties. The distinction between states that have accepted the jurisdiction of the Court and those that have not should be removed, in line with the recommendation in Section B of this commentary.**

Comment: As currently written, Article 87[79](4) could apply to either extradition requests to state parties from other state parties, or to state parties from states that are not parties to the treaty. With regard to requests from state parties, the requests of the Court should always take priority. In accordance with our view that the jurisdiction of the Court be limited to core crimes, and that such jurisdiction be fully accepted by states upon ratification or accession to the treaty with no additional "opt-in" requirement, the distinction between state parties and non-state parties should be removed.

---

[324] Article 52 of the International Law Commission's original draft statute provided that, if need be, the Court may request that a state take necessary provisional measures, pending a formal request for assistance.

The reference in Article 87[79](4) to prioritizing "as far as possible" is ambiguous. It should be clarified that, regardless of whether it is possible to prioritize a request from the Court over requests from non-state parties, requests from the Court should always take precedence over requests from state parties.

RELATIONSHIP OF THE STATUTE TO OTHER INTERNATIONAL INSTRUMENTS

Article 87[79](4): Parallel requests from the Court and states

- **Recommendation: The statute should state that compliance with the Court's requests will satisfy the requirements of preexisting treaties between state parties. It should further avoid the possibility of states seeking to rely on subsequent international agreements as a justification for non-compliance. To this end, the statute should be amended to explicitly provide that the obligations of the treaty--with respect to transfer and arrest of an accused or other matters of cooperation--may not be modified by subsequent distinct agreements entered into by state parties.**

Comment: It should be expressed that compliance with the Court's statute will satisfy the requirements of preexisting treaties between state parties. This is, however, insufficient to ensure that subsequent treaties will not be interposed as obstacles to compliance in arrest and transfer and other cooperation matters. Under the Vienna Convention on the Law of Treaties, such bilateral modification of multilateral treaties is not allowed except by express provision of the multilateral treaty, or in the absence of a prohibition, where the modification will not affect the rights or obligations of other parties or does not imply derogation of a provision which would be incompatible with the effective execution of the object and purpose of the treaty as a whole.[325] As refusal to transfer an accused will of necessity defeat the purpose of bringing those accused of the most serious

---

[325] Article 41 of the Vienna Convention on the Law of Treaties provides that two or more parties to a multilateral treaty may conclude an agreement to modify the treaty only where the treaty so provides or the modification in question is not prohibited and "(I) does not affect the enjoyment by other Parties of their rights under the treaty or the performance of their obligations, or (ii) does not relate to a provision, derogation from which is incompatible with the effective execution of the object and purpose of the treaty as a whole." Without doubt, subsequently executed extradition or mutual assistance treaties that would obstruct the functioning of the International Criminal Court would violate such provisions.

international crimes to justice in an international forum, the statute include an express prohibition of agreements that would modify obligations in this regard.

DELAY TO THE TRANSFER OF PERSONS SOUGHT

Article 87[79](6): Delayed transfer on ground of national proceedings or sentences

- *Recommendation:* **Article 87[79](6), which deals with delay in surrendering a suspect on the basis that the person is being proceeded against on the national level or is serving a sentence "for a crime different from that for which surrender is sought," should be amended. The scope of this provision should be narrowed to situations where a suspect is being proceeded against for a crime that is within the jurisdiction of the Court, or of comparable gravity to the crimes within the Court's jurisdiction. In all other cases, the state party should agree to the temporary transfer. Finally, the requirement that the consent of the Court be obtained for any delay under the provisions of this article should be upheld.**

Comment: Since the ICC's jurisdiction should be limited to the most serious international crimes, its prosecutions should not be delayed, and thus compromised, by ongoing state investigations or prosecutions for lesser offenses. It is reasonable that the state proceeding with a lesser offence wait for the completion of the international trial, and important to bar the dilatory tactic of interposing investigations for relatively unimportant crimes.

Different considerations pertain to the situation where a state party is proceeding against an accused for crimes equal in magnitude to the core crimes in the Court's statute. In those cases, it is reasonable for the state party to have the option to conclude its proceeding before transfer. This situation will mainly arise in the rare case where, for example, a state is trying an accused of crimes against humanity and the Court wishes to prosecute war crimes or genocide. Where a state party is trying an accused for the same offense for which he is sought by the Court, the state party will be able to challenge the admissibility of the case before the Court.

The fact that an accused is serving a sentence imposed by a state party should not serve as a barrier to transfer for the purpose of investigation or trial. In these circumstances, the accused will be kept in custody during the time required for these proceedings, which can be counted as time served towards the completion of either the state sentence or any potential sentence imposed by the Court.

Finally, it is essential that the decision of whether postponement is justified under this article be, as with all provisions of the statute, ultimately a matter for determination by the ICC itself. We therefore urge retention of the square bracketed references to consent of the Court being required to postpone the surrender of the person sought.

REQUESTS FOR OTHER FORMS OF COOPERATION

Article 90[82](1): Requests from the Court

• **Recommendation: The list in Article 90[82] should be non-exhaustive as to the nature of the requests that may be made by the Court.**

Comment: The ICC will, as stated above, be entirely reliant on states for the discharge of its functions. As such, it must have sufficiently broad powers to ensure that it can request all measures that prove necessary for this purpose. This entails having the flexibility to make requests beyond those that may be anticipated at the time of drawing up the statute. Human Rights Watch therefore underscores the importance of the list of cooperation measures being non-exhaustive, as provided in paragraph (m) of this provision. The statute should retain such a reference to "any other types of assistance."

INFORMATION PROVIDED FOR THE PURPOSE OF GENERATING EVIDENCE ONLY

Article 90[82](6)

• **Recommendation: Article 90[82](6) provides that a state may transmit documents or information to the prosecutor on a confidential basis and the prosecutor can then use them solely for the purpose of generating new evidence, unless the state consents. The statute should vest in the Court the final authority to determine how to use information made available to it. A state's request for confidentiality should not preclude the Court from using evidence for purposes other than generating new evidence, should the interests of justice so demand. In such cases, Option 2 of Article 71[64] will still require the Court to pay due regard to the national security of the state and give the state adequate opportunity to make representations to the Court.**

Comment: For the court to function fairly and effectively, it is extremely important that the prosecutor have access to the fullest information, and that states are encouraged to freely provide relevant information to the Court. At the same time, it is essential that the Court does not surrender ultimate authority to decide what the interests of justice demand in any particular case. For example, the Court must not be prevented from disclosing to the defense information critical to the preparation of a defense which the state has no legitimate interest in withholding.[326]

It should be noted that Article 90[82](6) imposes no restriction on the reasons why a state might wish evidence to be kept confidential. If national security interests are involve, then Option 2 of Article 71 would apply, requiring the Court to pay to the due regard to the state's claims of national security and granting the state an opportunity to make representations before the Court regarding its concerns. Genuine national security concerns of the state can be further addressed challenges to requests for cooperation, as outlined in the forgoing recommendations, or challenges to disclosure, set out below. Legitimate safety concerns may be addressed through applications to protect witnesses under Article 68[61] below. In each case, the Court must retain the authority to make the final determination on how the information is to be used.

The statute must guard against the situation wherein a state, by surrendering information or evidence under this article, can control the manner in which the information is used. This would clearly expose the Court to unacceptable political manipulation.[327] If a state could limit the Court's use of important information for any or no particular reason, this would entirely undermine the obligatory nature of full cooperation and compliance with the Court's requests, as provided for in this part of the statute.

NON APPLICABILITY OF THE RULE OF SPECIALITY

Article 92[84]: Rule of speciality

• **Recommendation: The rule of speciality provides that an accused may only be prosecuted for the crime in consideration of which he or she was surrendered by a state, and that evidence provided by a state shall be used only for the purpose for which it was requested. In view of the extremely**

---

[326] See recommendation below.

[327] It is noted that where the Court wishes to disclose information to the accused, pursuant to Article 58[51], the state has the right to challenge that disclosure and seek an order of non-disclosure, under Article 58[51] (f).

limited jurisdiction of the Court, the rule of speciality is appropriate and Article 92[84] should be deleted in its entirety.

Comment: Speciality has been viewed as an important source of protection of the rights of accused persons in the context of extradition, preventing requesting states from prosecuting surrendered individuals on charges totally unrelated to the request, that the surrendering state has not had the opportunity to evaluate. We believe that it is extremely unlikely the ICC will engage in abusive "fishing expeditions," and in view of the very limited scope of crimes we advocate placing under its jurisdiction, the danger of abusive prosecution is minimal.

This speciality provision could politicize the Court, by empowering a state to control or influence the way in which international prosecutions proceed. It would be unacceptable, for example, for a state to surrender evidence to be used in the prosecution of a national of state X, and yet bar the Court from using that evidence in the prosecution of a national of state Y, with which the surrendering state enjoys friendlier relations. The Court should not be fashioned with an inherent susceptibility to political manipulation.

Finally, the Court's jurisdiction should be limited to core crimes of the most serious character: crimes against humanity, genocide, and serious breaches of the laws and customs of war. In any given situation where such charges are likely, the abuses that would give rise to them are likely to share a common nexus of fact. The practice of the *ad hoc* tribunals has shown that after transfer, the tribunal is likely to have substantially more information than it had prior to the request. It serves little valid purpose to require the Court to prosecute a suspect on war crimes alone when subsequent information shows that he or she is also responsible for genocide or crimes against humanity.

SECTION O: COMPENSATION TO THE ACCUSED

Article 84 [53(8) and 50]

- *Recommendation:* **The right to compensation in the wake of arrest or detention which violates the statute or internationally recognized human rights standards, or a miscarriage of justice, should be retained.**

Comment: Article 84 of the current draft makes appropriate provision for compensation of the accused in the event of wrongful arrest or a miscarriage of justice.[328] The right of the accused to compensation in these circumstances is enshrined in broadly ratified human rights instruments.

Article 9(5) of the International Covenant on Civil and Political Rights (ICCPR), provides: "Anyone who has been a victim of unlawful arrest or detention shall have an enforceable right to compensation." Article 14 of the ICCPR provides that: "When a person has by a final decision been convicted of a criminal offence and when subsequently his conviction has been reversed or he has been pardoned on the ground that a new or newly discovered fact shows conclusively that there has been a miscarriage of justice, the person who has suffered punishment as a result of such conviction shall be compensated according to law, unless it is proved that the non-disclosure of the unknown fact in time is wholly or partly attributable to him."[329]

If the ICC were to fall short of these well-established standards, its legitimacy and its credibility would be undermined. While details regarding compensation could be set out in the Rules of Procedure of the Court, the principle for the statute should reflect the above provision. Delegates should ensure that the currently bracketed text dealing with the right to compensation for accused persons is retained in the final version of the ICC statute.

---

[328] This right to compensation should be reflected in the wording of Article 60(9) [53(8)] of the draft statute which provides that where the Presidency or Pretrial Chamber decides that an arrest or detention was unlawful, the Presidency "*may* award compensation [emphasis added]." The language should be imperative, providing that compensation *will* be provided in these circumstances.

[329] Consistent with our recommendations in the section dealing with "applicable law", the reference to "in accordance with law" would refer to the statute and, in this case, the Rules of the Court, as well as relevant international law.

SECTION P: FINANCING OF THE ICC

Introduction

The provisions on the financing of the Court should be governed by the following principles. Firstly, the ICC must be an independent judicial body and, so far as possible, be free from external interference in the exercise of its functions. Secondly, ICC must be adequately financed, and equipped with professional staff of the highest caliber. Thirdly, funding should come from a solid and predictable source. Finally, the Court must be capable of establishment without delay.

Article 104: Funds of the Court

* **Recommendation:** **Provide for the secure and sufficient financing of the Court, free from susceptibility to political manipulation and control. While not a perfect option, financing from the budget of the United Nations is the best way to meet these objectives.**

Comment: Adequate funding and qualified, professional staff is essential if the Court is to efficiently discharge its critical mandate.[330] The current text of Article 104 contains three options: firstly, that the Court be funded from contributions by states parties, secondly, that it be funded out of the regular budget of the U.N., or thirdly, that it be funded by combination of the two previous options, with an initial phase during which the expenses shall be borne by the U.N.

Funding from U.N. assessments is entirely appropriate given the universal nature and mandate of the Court to prosecute crimes of concern to the international community as a whole. Strong financial and other links with the U.N., if coupled with the necessary safeguards for its independence, would enhance the international standing of the Court.

---

[330] Undoubtedly, the costs involved in the establishment and operation of this Court will be substantial. For a study of the financial implications, see, generally, Tom Warrick, "Organization of the International Criminal Court: Administrative and Financial Issues" in *The International Criminal Court: Observations and Issues before the 1997-98 Preparatory Committee and Administrative and Financial Implications* (Association Internationale de Droit Penal, 1997).

159

Whether the ICC emerges as a treaty body or a an independent international organization[331], it critical is that the funding of the Court come from the regular U.N. budget of the United Nations. Treaty bodies can be and generally are funded from the U.N. budget, that they are supported by a secretariat provided by the U.N.[332] The establishment of the Court as an independent international organization does not preclude U.N. financing and must not be used to justify burdening state parties with the costs of this international institution.

The proposal that state parties meet the costs of the Court is problematic on several grounds.[333] Firstly, making states parties bear the heavy financial burden of the Court's expenses would be a disincentive to ratification. states must be encouraged to ratify, not penalized for doing so. states with more limited financial resources must not be in any way impeded from becoming parties to the treaty or from bringing complaints to the Court, on the basis of their lesser ability to pay.

Secondly, attempts to finance bodies entirely from contributions by states parties have proven unworkable in the past.[334] While financing by the U.N. will not entirely remove the issue from the political arena, it is preferable to funding by states parties. Funding by states parties would subject the Court to control by a smaller number of individual states, which could paralyze its operation through the nonpayment of dues.

Finally, the proposal that states should pay for the complaints they choose to lodge also raises serious concerns. States should not be required to pay for lodging good faith complaints.[335] The rationale underlying this proposal is entirely misconceived. Given that such complaints should not be made in the interest of the state itself, but in the interests of international justice, states should be encouraged

---

[331]See Article 2 of the draft statute

[332] For example, the Committee against Torture, created by the Convention Against Torture and Other Cruel, Inhuman or Degrading Treatment or Punishment, Article 17; GA Res. 39/46, UN GAOR, 39th session, Supp. No. 51, p.197.

[333] These concerns are relevant to Options 1 and 3.

[334] This was the experience of certain bodies, such as the Committee on the Elimination of Racial Discrimination and Committee against Torture. While they began their existence funded by states parties, crises brought about by nonpayment lead them to transfer to the regular budget of the U.N.

[335] Other proposals that have been made include, for example, the U.S. proposal to the ad hoc committee in 1995, which supported funding from state parties, states responsible for bringing complaints (or the Security Council when it lodges a complaint), and voluntary contributions.

to make complaints, not financially penalized for doing so. Providing for U.N. financing would ensure that international justice is accessible to all states and their citizens, regardless of their financial means.

SECTION Q: FINAL CLAUSES

SETTLEMENT OF DISPUTES
Article 108[91]

• **Recommendation: The Court, and not the Assembly of state parties, should have competence over all disputes relating to the interpretation or application of this statute.**

Comment: Article 108[91] deals with the settlement of disputes between state parties relating to judicial activities and to the interpretation or application of the statute. Option 2 proposes that disputes "relating to the interpretation or application of this statute...shall be referred to the Assembly of states parties." This proposal would gravely undermine the role of the Court and allow state parties to usurp its judicial functions. Giving the Court competence over disputes relating to its judicial activities, and to the interpretation and application of the statute, is essential to the integrity of the statute and the independence and credibility of the ICC.

RESERVATIONS

Article 109[92]

• **Recommendation: The ICC statute should prohibit reservations.**

Comment: Article 109[92] includes options[336] which would permit reservations to the ICC statute.[337] Reservations would undermine the force and moral authority behind the treaty and weaken the nature of the obligations embodied in it.[338]

---

[336] These options were added during the March-April 1998 Preparatory Committee.

[337] This comment relates to reservations, which "...exclude or modify the legal effect of certain provisions of the treaty in their application to that State." (Article 2(1)(d) of the Vienna Convention on the Law of Treaties, U.N. Doc.A/Conf.39/27). As such, they should be distinguished from interpretative declarations that do not purport to exclude or modify the legal effect of the treaty but simply declare a state's interpretation, which have no legal consequences. D.W. Bowett, "Reservations to a Non-Restricted Multilateral Treaties," *British Yearbook of International Law*, vol.48, pp.67-8.

[338] Human Rights Committee, *General Comment on Issues Relating to Reservations Made Upon Ratification or Accession to the Covenant or the Optional Protocols thereto or in Relation to Article 41 of the Covenant* ("General Comment 24") para.1: "It is important for States Parties to know exactly what obligations they, and other

162

The problems associated with reservations were illustrated in a General Comment by the Human Rights Committee on reservations to the International Covenant on Civil and Political Rights.[339] As of November 1, 1994, 46 of the 127 States Parties to the International Covenant on Civil and Political Rights had, between them, entered 150 reservations to their acceptance of the obligations of the Covenant. The Committee notes: "The number of reservations, their content and their scope may undermine the effective implementation of the Covenant and tend to weaken respect for the obligations of States Parties."[340] Delegates are urged not to potentially undermine the role of the ICC by permitting reservations.

While reservations may encourage broader ratification of the statute, near-universal ratification is neither desirable, in and of itself, nor is it essential to the effective functioning of the Court. What is essential is that the Court meet certain benchmarks of fairness and independence, and that the obligations of states parties *vis-a-vis* the Court be clear. Human Rights Watch therefore supports the prohibition on reservations, as proposed in Option 1.

With regard to the option to have no provision whatsoever on reservations, in the absence of any provision reservations would have to be interpreted in accordance with the Vienna Convention on the Law of Treaties. The Vienna Convention's prohibition on reservations that are "incompatible with the object and purpose of the treaty" would not be sufficient to protect the integrity of the ICC statute. The issue of whether a reservation is compatible with the object and purpose of the treaty will only be raised when another state lodges an objection to the reservation. In practice, state will often decline to object to reservations for a variety of reason.

In this context, the Human Rights Committee has noted that, given the reluctance of states to lodge complaints against other states, "[i]t necessarily falls to the Committee to determine whether a specific reservation is compatible with the object and purpose of the Covenant."[341] If the ICC statute allows for reservations, then the Court must have the competence to determine the permissibility of the reservations automatically, without being dependant on any state to challenge the

---

States Parties, have in fact undertaken. And the Committee, in the performance of its duties ... must know whether a State is bound by a particular obligation or to what extent."

[339] The International Covenant on Civil and Political Rights (ICCPR), adopted December 16, 1966, (U.N. G.A. Resolution 2200 A XXI) 999 UN Treaty Series 171, and entered into force on May 23, 1976.

[340] Human Rights Committee, "General Comment 24", ibid.

[341] Ibid, paras.17-18.

reservation in order to do so. In the case of the ICCPR, the Human Rights Committee has noted the absence of a state objection to a reservation should not be construed as an acceptance.

EARLY ACTIVATION OF PRINCIPLES AND RULES OF THE STATUTE

Article 113[96 bis]

- **Recommendation: Retain the provision providing that states that have signed the statute shall refrain from acts that would defeat its object and purpose, with a view to accelerating the achievement of the shared goal of establishing the Court.**

Comment: Article 113[96 bis] emphasizes the important principle enshrined in the Vienna Convention on the Law of International Treaties that states which have signed a treaty are obliged to refrain from acts which would defeat the object and purpose of the treaty.[342] Although technically unnecessary, this principle bears explicit mention. Article 113[96 bis] also recognizes that signatory states have a responsibility to work towards the early establishment of the Court.

RATIFICATION

Article 114[97](1)

- **Recommendation 1: The entry into force of the statute should not be delayed until the completion of the Rules of Procedure and Evidence.**

Comment: Delaying the entry into force of the statute until the Rules of Procedure and Evidence have been completed serves no purpose and will have the practical and extremely undesirable effect of delaying the establishment of the ICC. The proposal that "This Statute shall enter into force [following the completion of the Rules of Procedure and Evidence]..." should be therefore opposed.

---

[342] See Vienna Convention, Article 18(a): "A State is obliged to refrain from acts which would defeat the object and purpose of a treaty when...it has signed the treaty or has exchanged instruments constituting the treaty subject to ratification, acceptance or approval, until it shall have made its intention clear not to become a party to the treaty."

- *Recommendation 2:* **The number of ratifications specified as pre-requisite to the entry in force of the treaty should not be so high as to result in undue delay in the establishment of the Court.**

Comment: The atrocities of recent history cry out for the early establishment of an independent and effective International Criminal Court. If widespread ratification for an effective and credible ICC is not achieved immediately, however, it should not hamper the Court from being established and being able to begin to carry out its crucial mandate.

The statute should require the lowest of the proposed number of state ratifications necessary for the treaty's entry into force. Delegates should avoid any provision which would risk repetition of the experience of other treaties whose effect was paralyzed at the outset by the requirement of a high number of ratifying states. For example, United Nations Convention on the Law of the Sea required sixty ratifications.[343] The result was that it did not enter into force for 12 years, until 1994. A high number of required ratifications should not be allowed to cause inordinate delays in establishing the Court.

Moreover, given the nature of the Court's jurisdiction and the urgency of the situation that the Court is being established to address, a lower number of ratifications is, in our view, appropriate. Humanitarian treaties, given the nature of their subject matter, generally require very few ratifications to enter into force; the Protocols Additional to the Geneva Conventions (Protocols I and II), for example, required only two.[344] The 1994 Inter-American Convention on the Forced Disappearance of Persons similarly required ratification by only two states to enter into force.

---

[343] United Nations Convention on the Law of the Sea, opened for signature December 10, 1982, U.N. Doc. A/CONF.62/122 (1982), reprinted in *Official Text of the U.N. Convention on the Law of the Sea*, U.N. Sales No. E.83 V.5 (1983).

[344] The Protocol Additional to the Geneva Conventions of 12 August 1949, and Relating to the Protection of Victims of Non-International Armed Conflicts (Protocol II), and the Protocol Additional to the Geneva Conventions of 12 August 1949, and Relating to the Protection of Victims of International Armed Conflicts (Protocol I), provide at Articles 23(1) and Article 95 respectively: *"this Protocol shall enter into force six months after two instruments of ratification or accession have been deposited."* Both Protocols were adopted on June 8, 1977 and entered into force eighteen months later.

The Genocide Convention required twenty ratifications to enter into force,[345] as did the Conventional Weapons Convention,[346] the Torture Convention[347] and the Convention on the Rights of the Child[348]; the latter two treaties established bodies to monitor observance of the obligations assumed in the treaties. The objectives of the ICC treaty--and the urgency surrounding them--have much in common with the objectives underlying human rights and humanitarian law treaties.

In certain treaties, wide ratification is essential to achieve the treaty's purpose. The instrument establishing the ICC is not such a treaty. With each effective investigation and prosecution of genocide, crimes against humanity or serious war crimes, the Court's existence will have been justified. It can begin to achieve its goals even with relatively few ratifications. States can and will accede to the treaty over time. As the Court's reputation develops and the interest of states and the international community becomes apparent, support will increase. The ICC's ability to carry out its mandate should not be paralyzed by the often lengthy internal procedures prerequisite to ratification in a number of states.

As the Court ought, in our view, to be funded out of the regular budget of the U.N., there is no financial necessity to have a large number of ratifying states in order to share the initial burden.

---

[345] The Convention on the Prevention and Punishment of the Crime of Genocide (Genocide Convention), December 9, 1948, U.N. G.A. Resolution 260 A (III), Article 13, required twenty ratifications and entered into force in thirteen months.

[346] The Convention on Prohibitions or Restrictions on the Use of Certain Conventional Weapons which May Be Deemed to be Excessively Injurious or to Have Indiscriminate Effects, adopted at Geneva, October 10, 1980.

[347] The Convention Against Torture and Other Cruel, Inhuman or Degrading Treatment or Punishment (Torture Convention), December 10, 1984, U.N. G.A. Resolution 39/46, Article 27(1), required twenty ratifications and entered into force in two and a half years.

[348] The Convention on the Rights of the Child, November 20, 1989, Article 49(1) required twenty ratifications and entered into force in ten months.